Name_____

The Body Syste...

The human body is made of many systems that work together in groups. Label the different body systems in each group.

Movement group

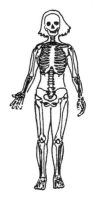 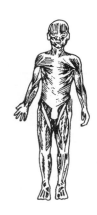

Control group

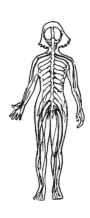 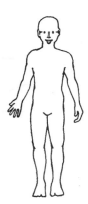 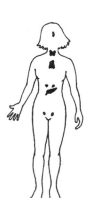

_____ _____ _____ _____ _____

Energy group

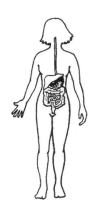 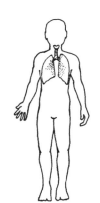 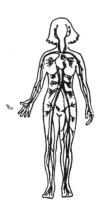 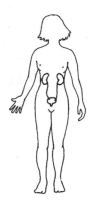

_____ _____ _____ _____

circulatory	digestive	endocrine
muscular	nervous	respiratory
sensory	·skeletal	urinary

1

Body Parts

Label the parts of the body.

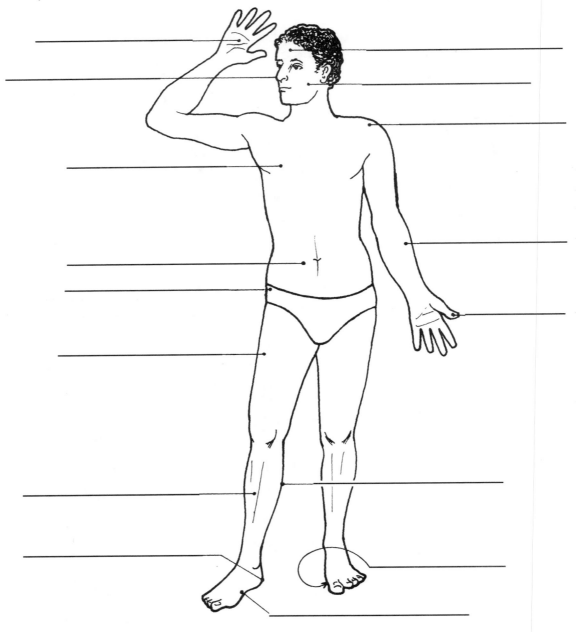

abdomen	calf	cheek	chest
forearm	forehead	heel	hip
instep	nose	palm	shin
shoulder	sole	thigh	thumb

The Skeletal System

Label the skeleton with the common and scientific names of each bone.

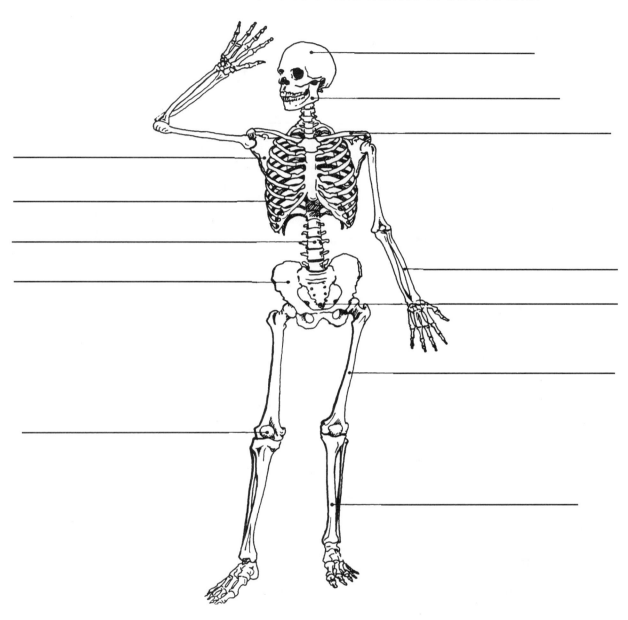

Common Name (Scientific Name)

backbone (vertebrae)	collarbone (clavicle)	hip bone (pelvis)
jawbone (mandible)	kneecap (patella)	lower arm bone (radius)
rib (rib)	shoulder blade (scapula)	shinbone (tibia)
skull (cranium)	tailbone (coccyx)	thighbone (femur)

Name_____

Head Bones

Label the bones that are found in the head and neck.

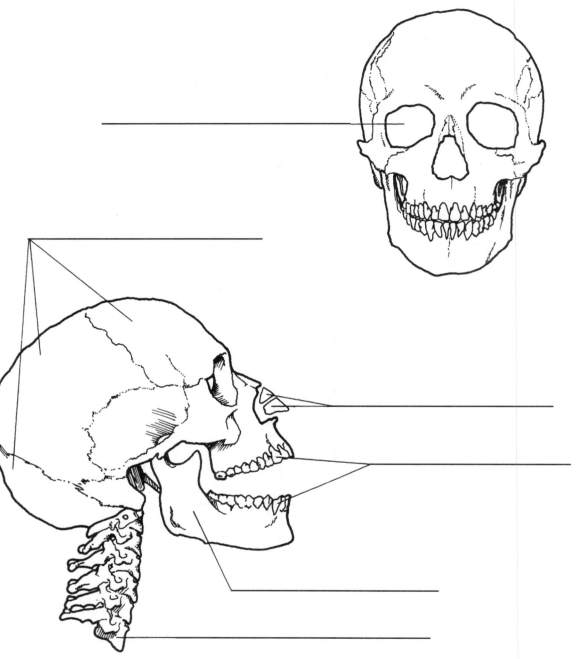

eye socket	jawbone (mandible)
nose cartilage	skull bones
teeth	vertebrae

Kinds of Joints

The place where two or more bones meet is called a **joint**. Joints are either movable or immovable. There are four kinds of movable joints: **hinge**, **pivot**, **gliding**, and **ball-and-socket**.

Label the three kinds of joints shown. List examples of where each kind of joint is found.

Kind of Joint	Joint	Man-Made Equal	Example
_____			_____ _____
_____			_____ _____
_____		(no man-made equal)	_____

elbow	hip	knee
shoulder	spine	wrist

Joints in the Body

Label each type of joint on the skeleton. Some words may be used more than once.

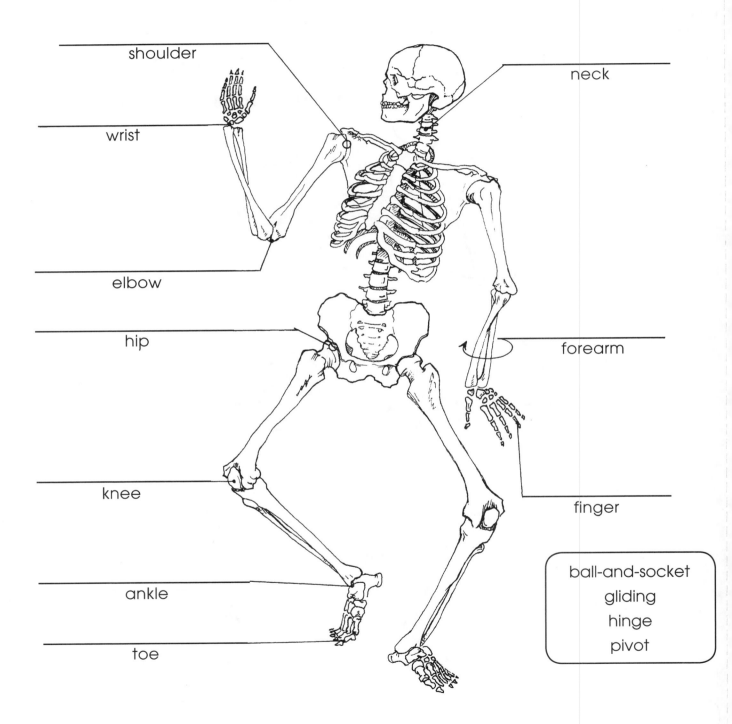

shoulder _____

wrist _____

elbow _____

hip _____

knee _____

ankle _____

toe _____

neck _____

forearm _____

finger _____

ball-and-socket
gliding
hinge
pivot

Bones

Label the parts of the long bone in the diagram.

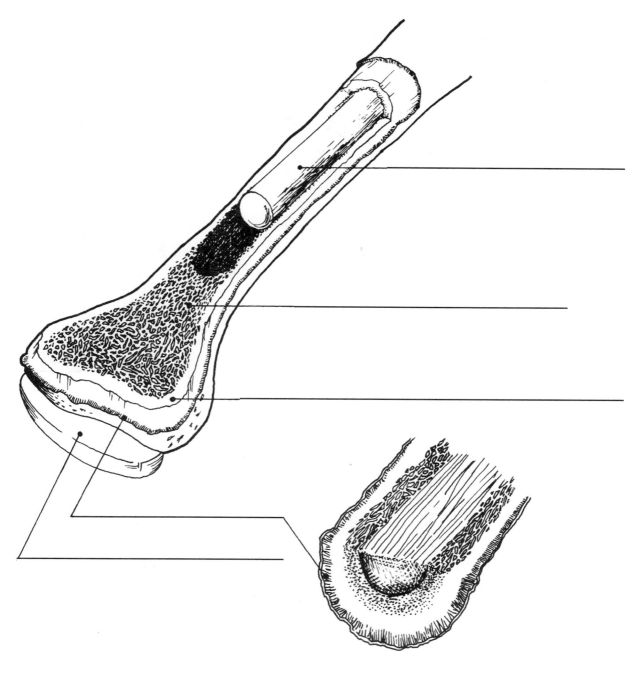

calcified bone	cartilage
marrow	periosteum
spongy bone	

Breaks in Bones

A break in a bone is called a **fracture**. Some of the common types of fractures are pictured.

Label the different kinds of fractures.

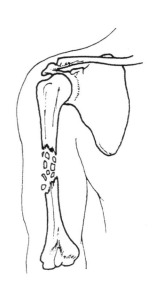 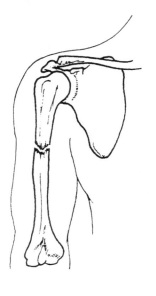 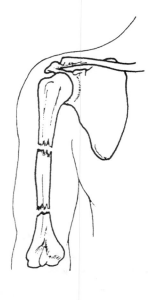

_____   _____   _____

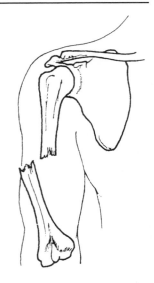 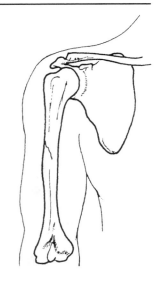 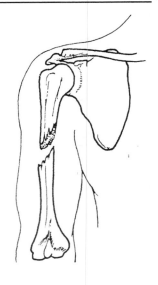

_____   _____   _____

| closed | comminuted | greenstick |
| multiple | open/compound | spiral |

The Backbone

Label the regions of the spine, or vertebral column.

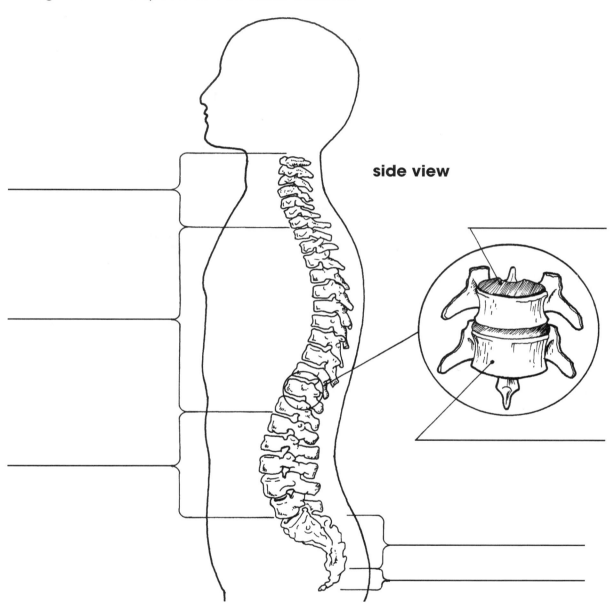

side view

Common Name (Scientific Name)

chest (thoracic region)

lower back (lumbar region)

pelvic girdle (sacral region)

vertebra

disc

neck (cervical region)

tailbone (coccygeal region)

The Hands and Feet

Label the bones of the hand and foot. Some words may be used more than once.

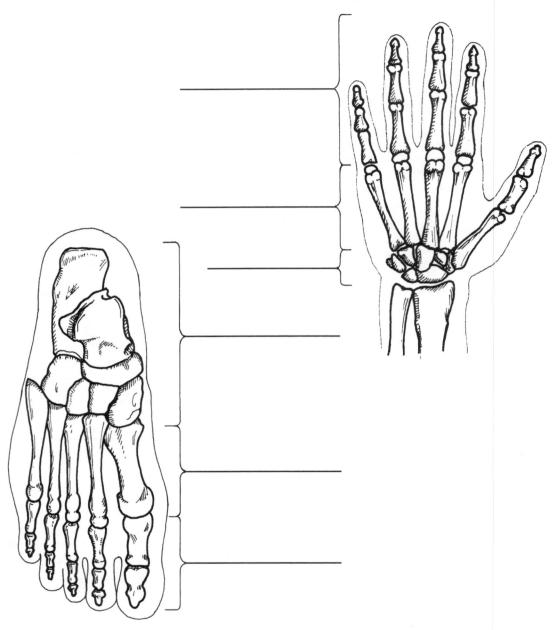

Common Name (Scientific Name)

ankle (tarsals)   digits (phalanges)

instep (metatarsals)   palm (metacarpals)

wrist (carpals)

Leg Bones

Label the different leg bones and regions.

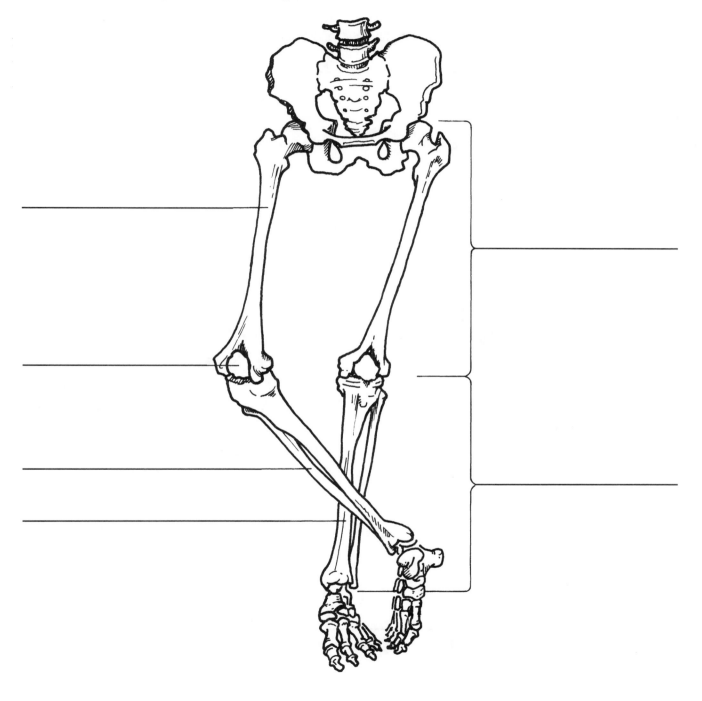

| femur | fibula | lower leg |
| patella | tibia | upper leg |

The Pelvis

The framework of bones that supports the lower part of the abdomen is called the **pelvis**. The male pelvis is heart-shaped and narrow. The female pelvis is much wider and flatter, with a larger central cavity to accomodate a fetus during pregnancy and childbirth.

Label the parts of the pelvis.

Male Pelvis   **Female Pelvis**

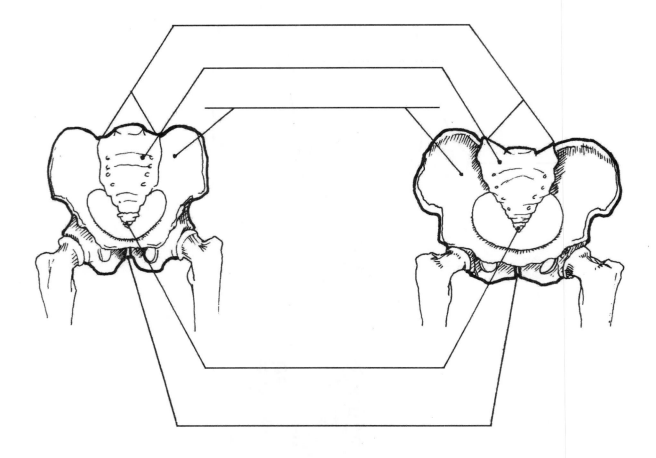

| coccyx | ilium/hipbone | interpubic joint |
| sacroiliac joints | sacrum | |

Bones of the Arm

Label the different arm bones and regions.

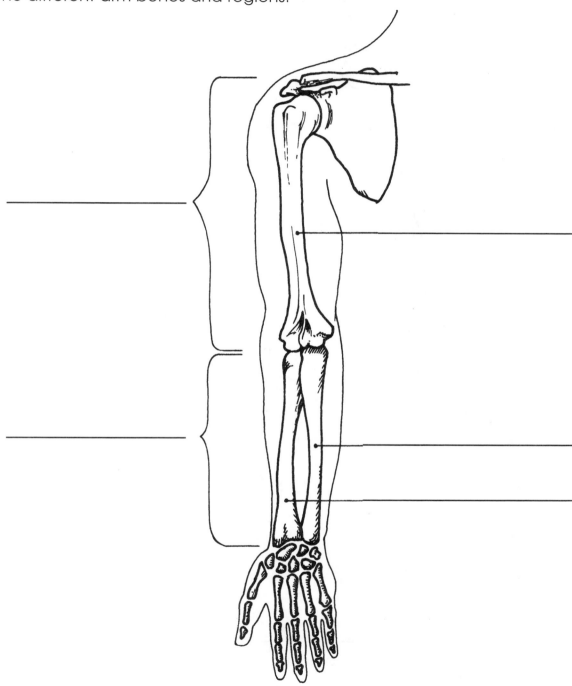

humerus	lower arm	radius
ulna	upper arm	

Bones Review

Cut out the skeleton and glue it together. Label the skeleton on the lines drawn on the bones using the words in the word bank.

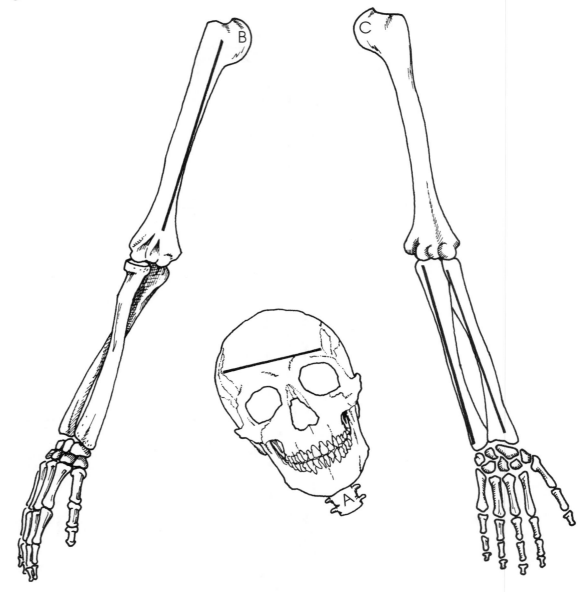

clavicle	cranium	femur
fibula	humerus	pelvis
radius	rib	scapula
spinal column	sternum	tibia
ulna		

Bones Review (con't.)

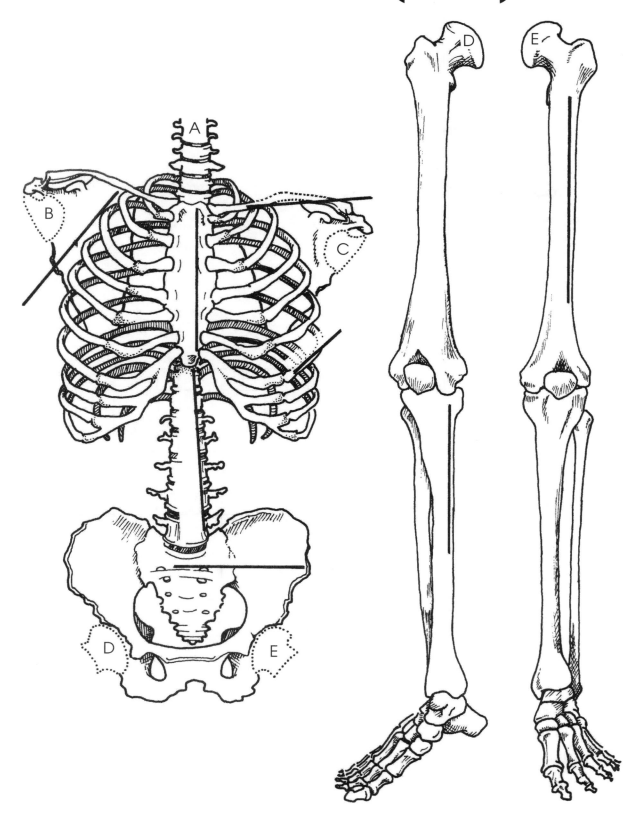

Skeletal System Crossword

Use the word bank to complete the puzzle.

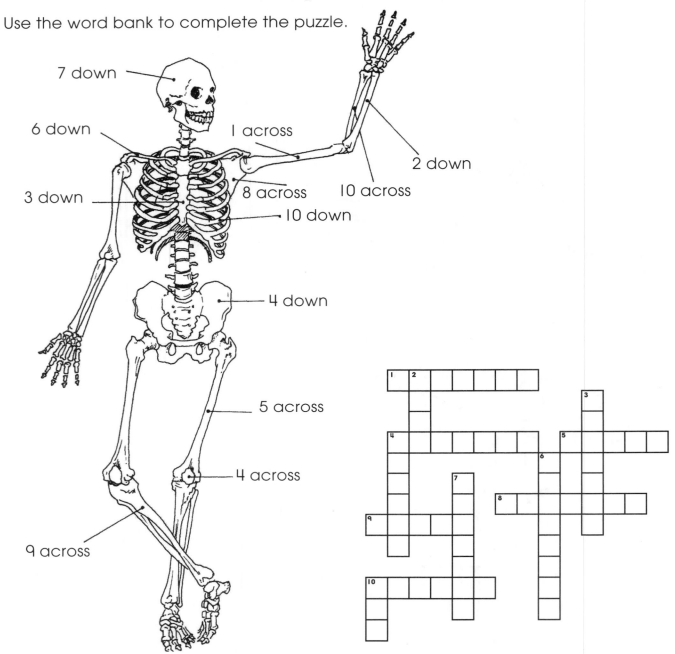

<table>
<tr><td>clavicle</td><td>cranium</td><td>femur</td></tr>
<tr><td>humerus</td><td>patella</td><td>pelvis</td></tr>
<tr><td>radius</td><td>rib</td><td>scapula</td></tr>
<tr><td>sternum</td><td>tibia</td><td>ulna</td></tr>
</table>

Inside Teeth

Teeth are made up of a number of layers. Label the layers and outside parts of the tooth.

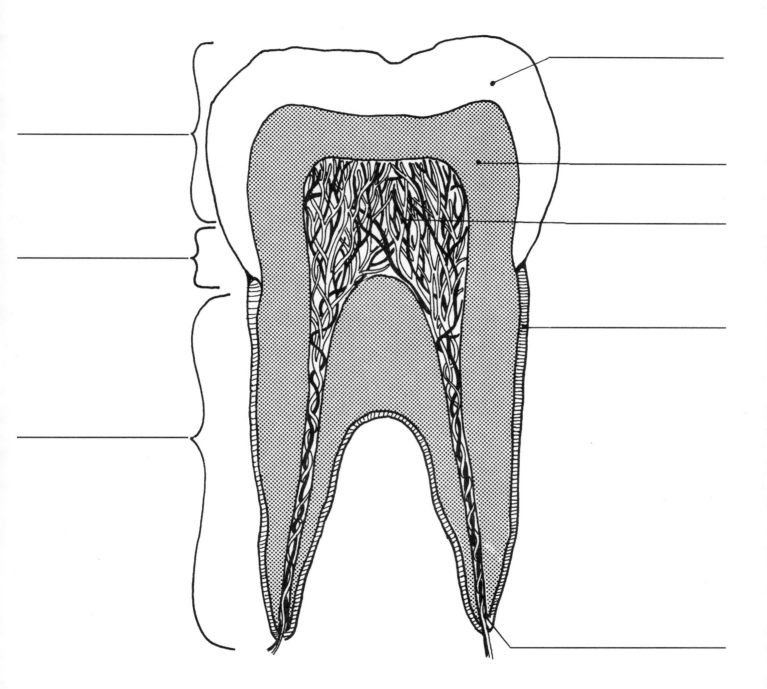

cementum	crown	dentin	enamel
neck	pulp	root	root canal

Bites

Each of the diagrams illustrates a different **bite**. The bite is the angle at which the upper and lower teeth meet.

Label the kind of bite found in each left-hand picture. Then, draw a line from the bite on the left to the corresponding profile on the right.

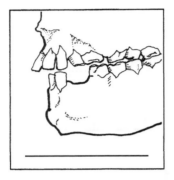

_____

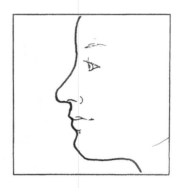

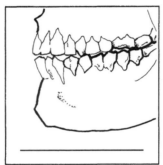

_____

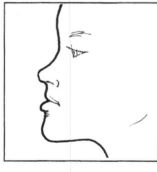

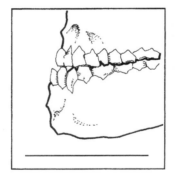

_____

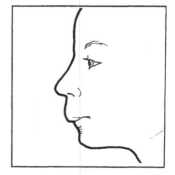

A dentist can correct an overbite or underbite by _____

_____.

| normal bite | overbite | underbite |

Kinds of Teeth

There are four kinds of teeth in the human mouth. Label the adult teeth. Some words may be used more than once.

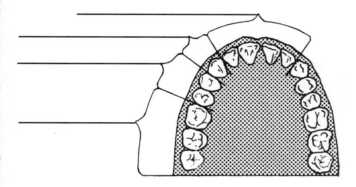

Adult upper

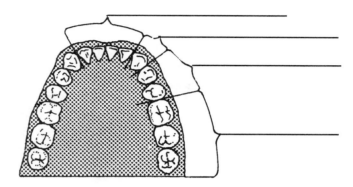

Adult lower

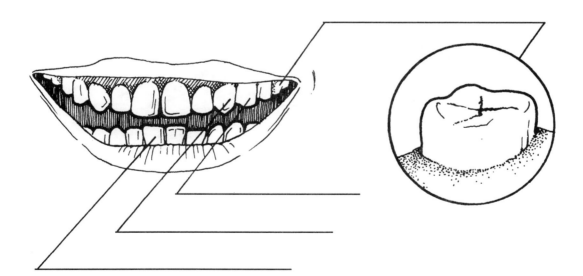

bicuspids (premolars)	canines	incisors	molars

Muscles

There are hundreds of muscle groups in the body. Label the muscles that appear on the surface of the body.

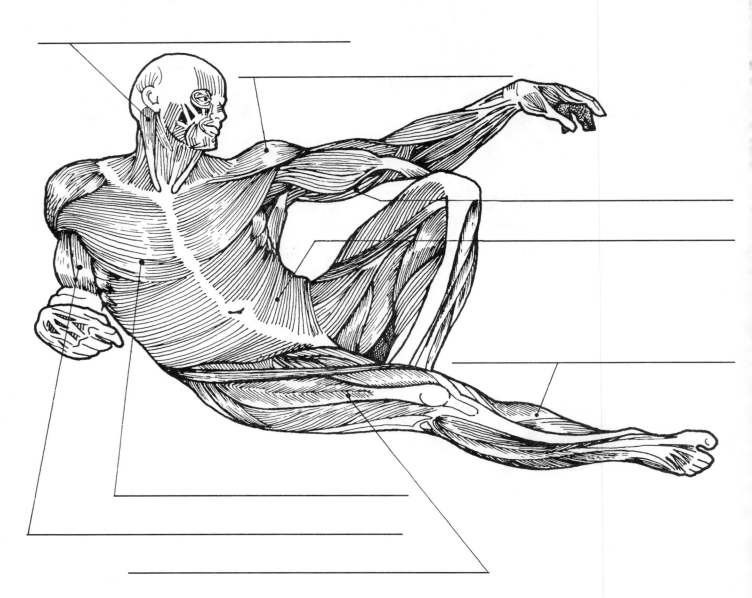

Common Name (Scientific Name)

biceps (biceps)

chest muscles (pectorals)

shoulder muscles (deltoids)

thigh muscles (quadriceps)

calf muscles (gastrocnemius)

head muscles (sternocleidomastoids)

stomach muscles (intercostals)

triceps (triceps)

Skeletal Muscles

Skeletal muscles are attached to the skeleton by **tendons**.

Label the parts of the arm.

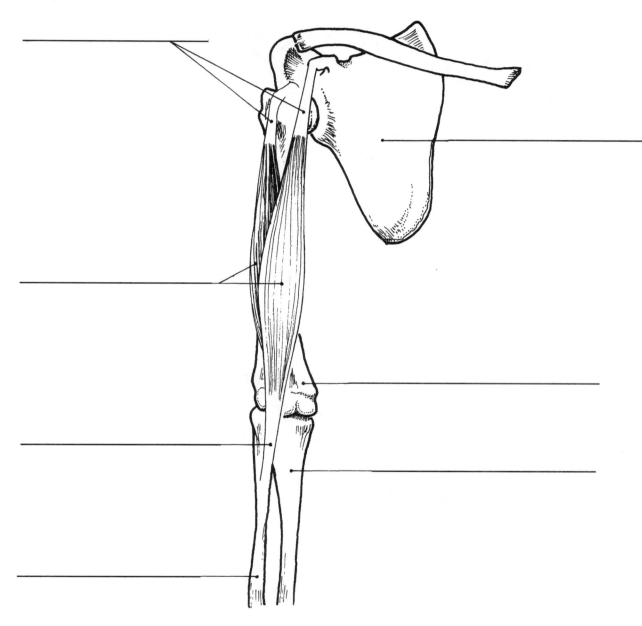

biceps muscle	humerus
radius	shoulder blade (scapula)
tendon or tendons	ulna

Muscle Types

Label the three different types of muscles and give an example of the kind of work they do. Then, label the muscle parts in the diagram. Some words may be used more than once.

A.

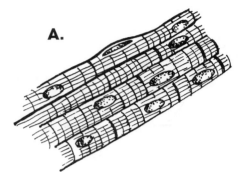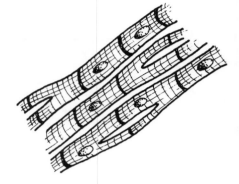

Type of Muscle

_____   _____   _____

Kind of Work

_____   _____   _____

B.

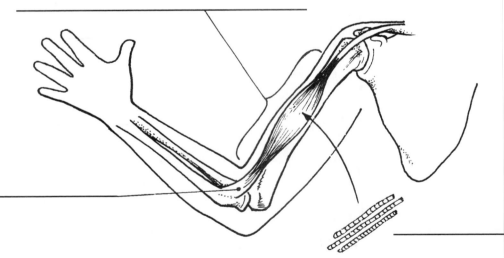

cardiac muscle	muscle group
muscle fiber	skeletal muscle
smooth muscle	tendon

Working Pairs

The muscles in both your upper arms and upper legs are very much alike. They both work in pairs to help raise and lower the limbs. Label the parts of each "working pair."

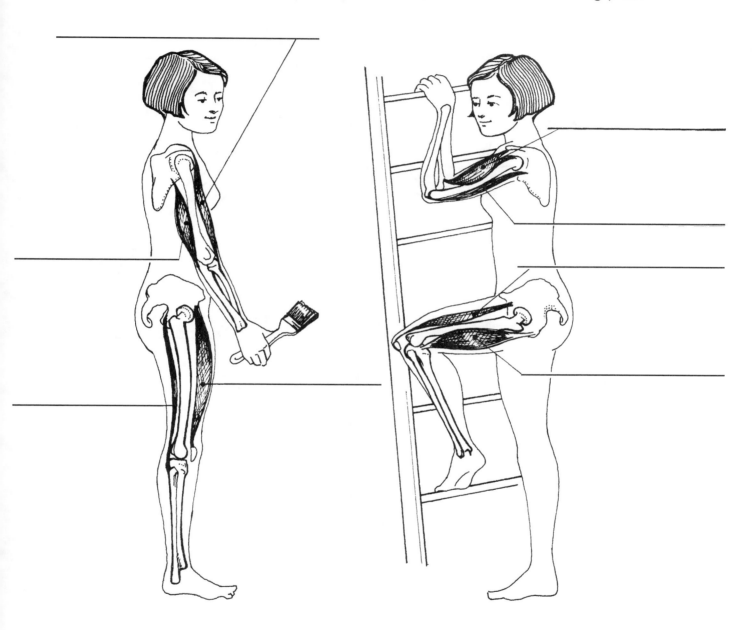

biceps contracted	biceps relaxed
hamstrings contracted	hamstrings relaxed
quadriceps contracted	quadriceps relaxed
triceps contracted	triceps relaxed

The Circulatory System

Label the parts of the circulatory system.

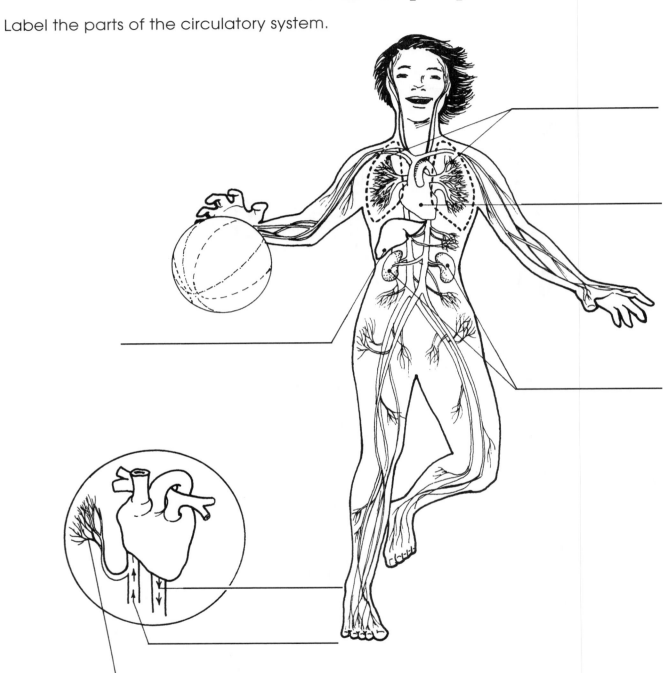

artery	capillaries	heart
kidneys	liver	lungs
vein		

Veins and Arteries

Arteries

Draw arrows on the arteries showing
the flow of blood away from the heart.

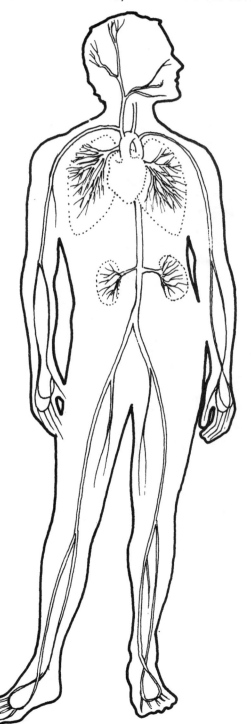

Veins

Draw arrows on the veins showing
the flow of blood back to the heart.

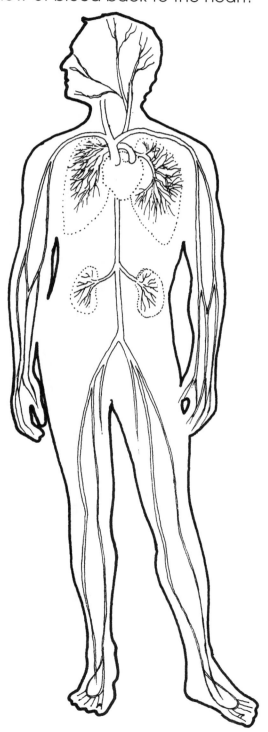

The Heart

Label the parts of the heart.

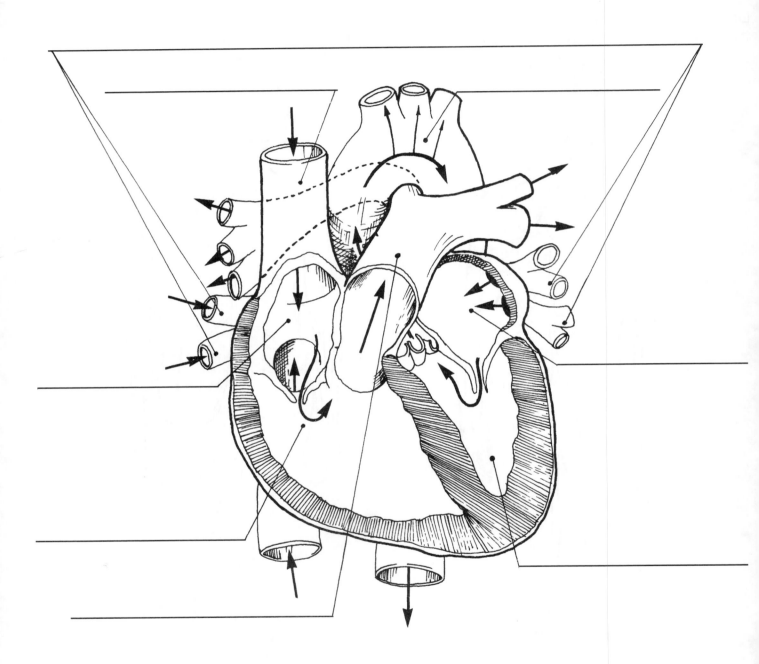

aorta	left atrium	left ventricle
pulmonary artery	pulmonary veins	right atrium
right ventricle	vena cava	

The Heart

The heart has the job of pumping blood to the parts of the body. Label the parts of the heart and the location of the flow of blood.

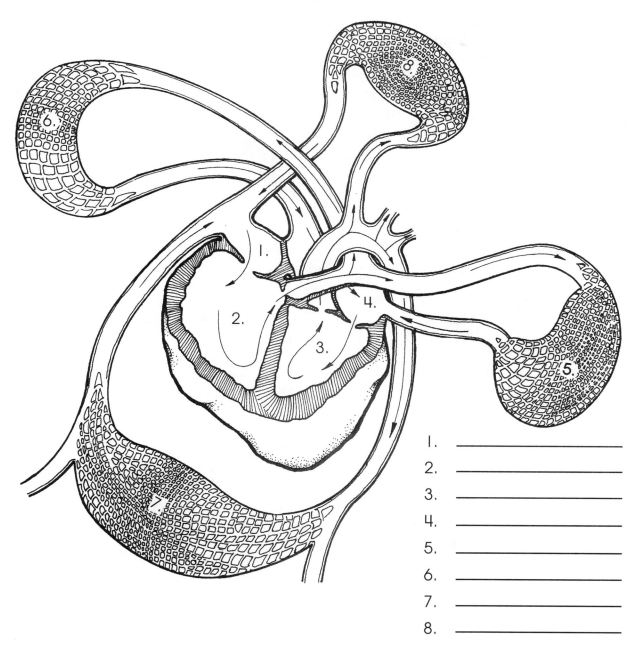

1. _____

2. _____

3. _____

4. _____

5. _____

6. _____

7. _____

8. _____

left atrium	left lung	left ventricle
lower body	right atrium	right lung
right ventricle	upper body	

Pressure Points

When a person is cut severely and begins to bleed, it is time for quick action. First aid for severe bleeding involves applying pressure over the wound. Sometimes, it is possible to press the artery above the wound against the bone behind it to stop the bleeding. This place is called a **pressure point**. A pressure point is also an excellent location to take a person's pulse.

Place an **X** on the pressure points behind the knee, in the bend of the elbow, on the inside of the thigh, on the neck, on top of the foot, and on the wrist.

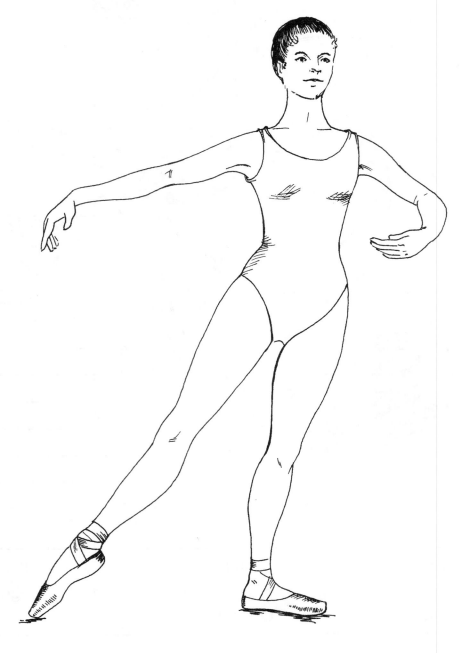

Name_____

Circulatory System Crossword

Use the word bank to complete the puzzle.

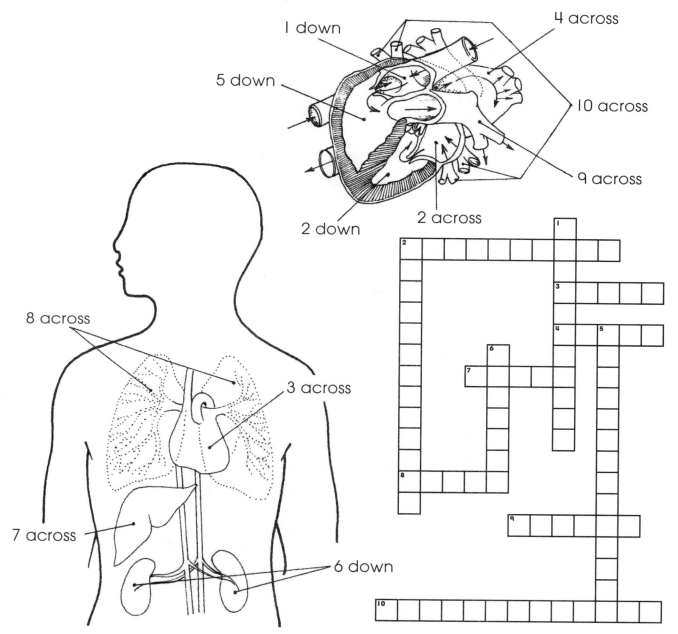

Word Bank:

aorta	artery	heart
kidneys	left atrium	left ventricle
liver	lungs	pulmonary vein
right atrium	right ventricle	

29

The Respiratory System

Label the parts of the respiratory system.

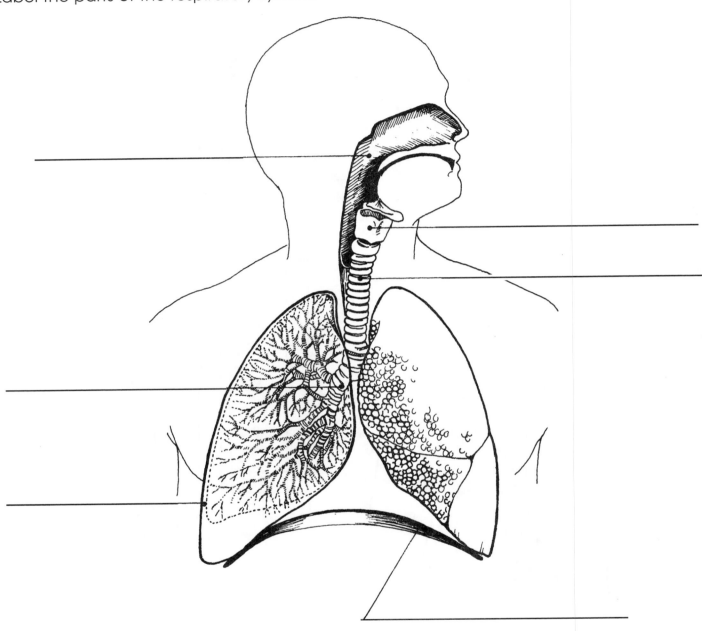

Common Name (Scientific Name)

bronchial tube (bronchial tube)   diaphragm (diaphragm)

lung cover (pleura)   throat (pharynx)

voice box (larynx)   windpipe (trachea)

The Lungs

Label the parts of the lungs.

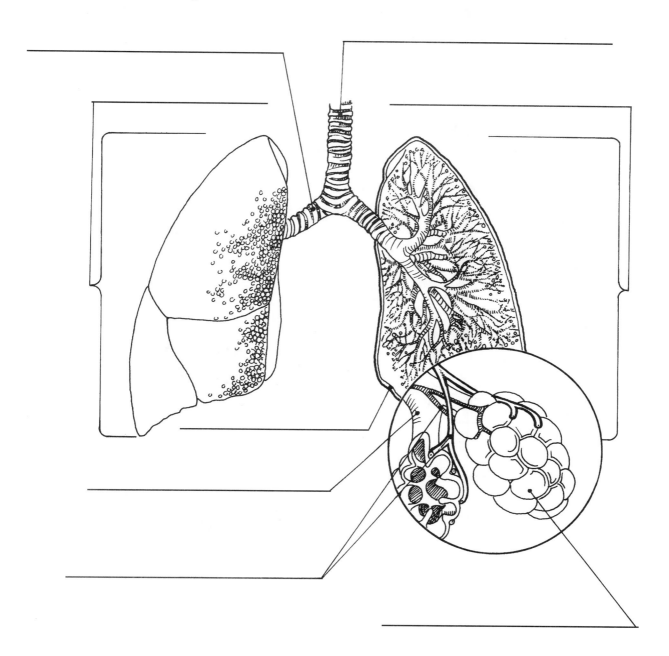

alveoli	bronchial tube
bronchiole	capillaries
left lung	pleura
right lung	trachea

Breathing

Humans breathe in and breathe out almost 20,000 times each day. Label these pictures **inhale** (breathing in) or **exhale** (breathing out). Label the other parts of the breathing process.

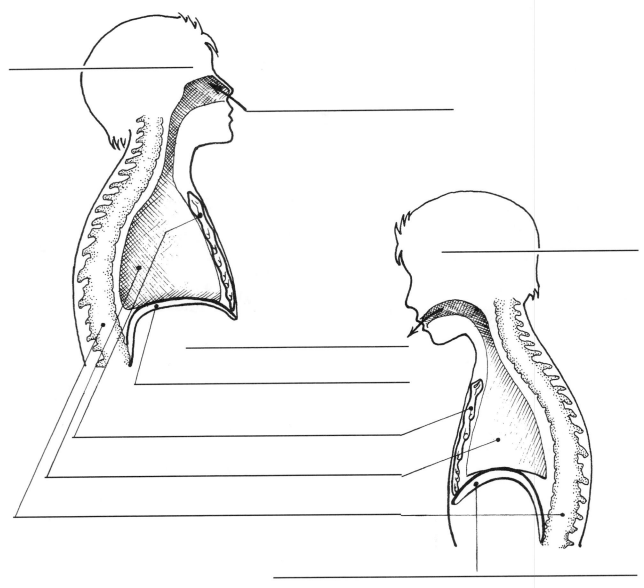

breastbone	carbon dioxide
contracted diaphragm	lung
oxygen	relaxed diaphragm
spine	

Respiratory System Crossword

Use the word bank to complete the puzzle.

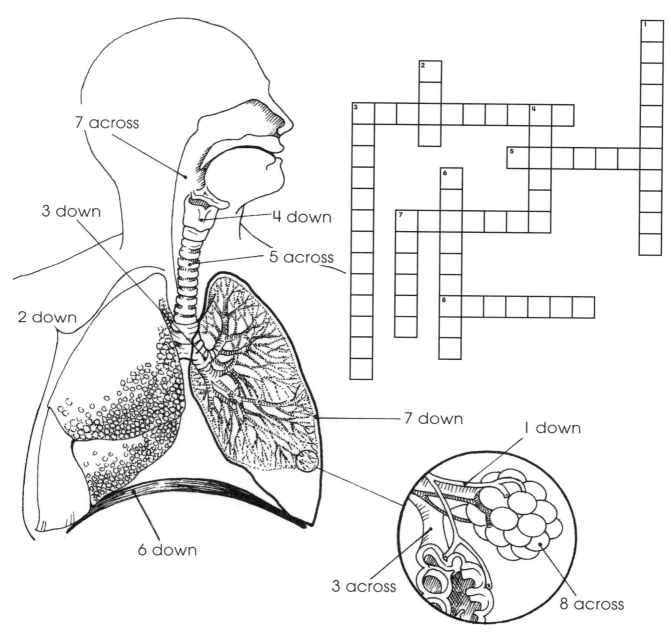

7 across

3 down

4 down

5 across

2 down

7 down

1 down

6 down

3 across

8 across

alveoli	bronchial tube	bronchioli
capillaries	diaphragm	larynx
lung	pharynx	pleura
trachea		

The Digestive System

Label the parts of the digestive system.

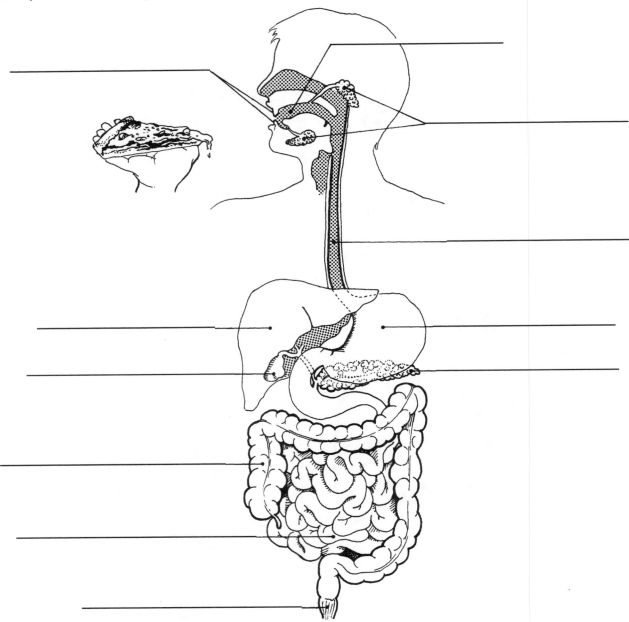

anus	esophagus	gallbladder
large intestine	liver	mouth
pancreas	salivary glands	small intestine
stomach	teeth	

The Alimentary Canal

The main part of the digestive system is the **alimentary canal**, a tube which starts at the mouth and travels through the body, ending at the anus.

Label the parts of the alimentary canal.

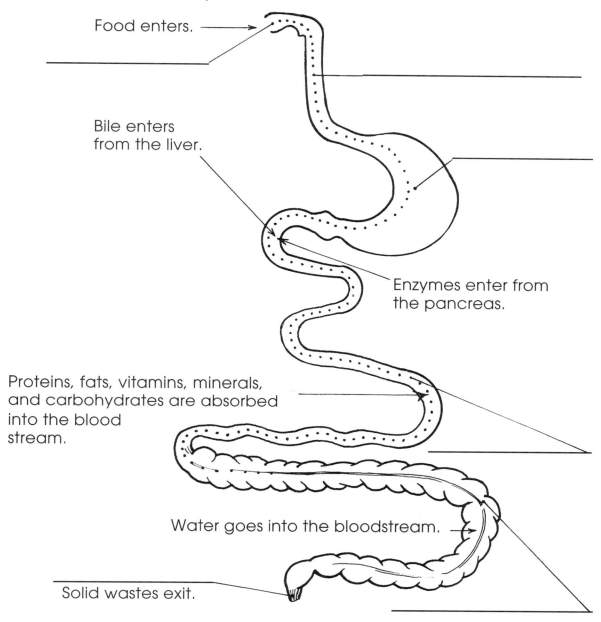

Food enters. ———→

_____

Bile enters
from the liver.

Enzymes enter from
the pancreas.

Proteins, fats, vitamins, minerals,
and carbohydrates are absorbed
into the blood
stream.

Water goes into the bloodstream. —→

Solid wastes exit.

| anus | esophagus | large intestine |
| mouth | small intestine | stomach |

The Stomach

The **stomach** is the widest part of the alimentary canal. The stomach has three layers of muscles that allow it to contract in different directions. The contracting motion mashes food and mixes it with digestive juices.

Label the parts of the stomach and the tubes leading into and out of the stomach.

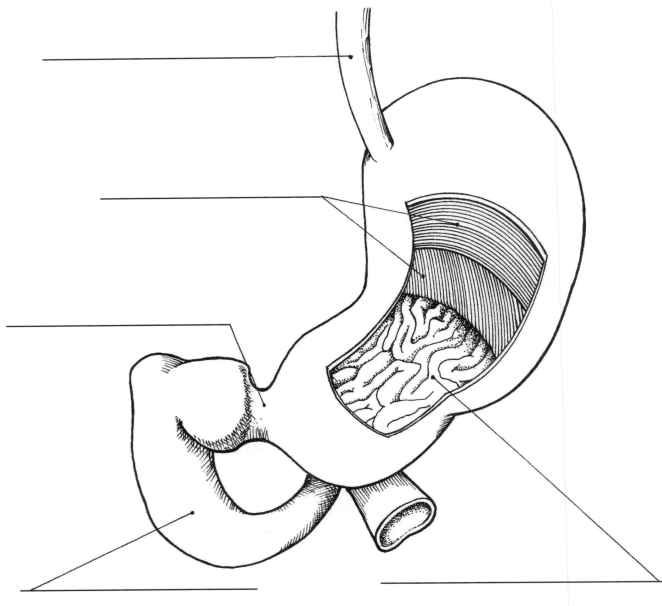

duodenum	esophagus	mucous membrane
muscle layers	sphincter	

Digestion in the Mouth

Label the parts of the digestive system located in and around the mouth.

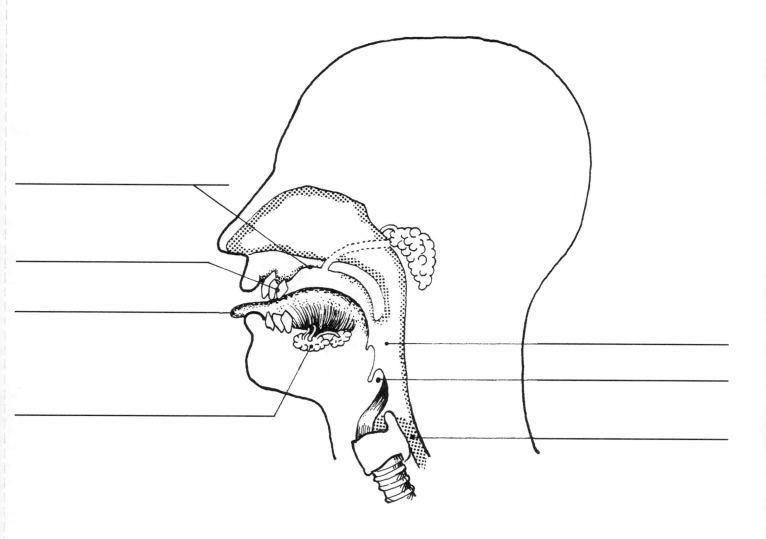

epiglottis	esophagus	palate
pharynx	salivary glands	teeth
tongue		

The Pancreas, Liver, and Gallbladder

Label these organs that aid in digestion.

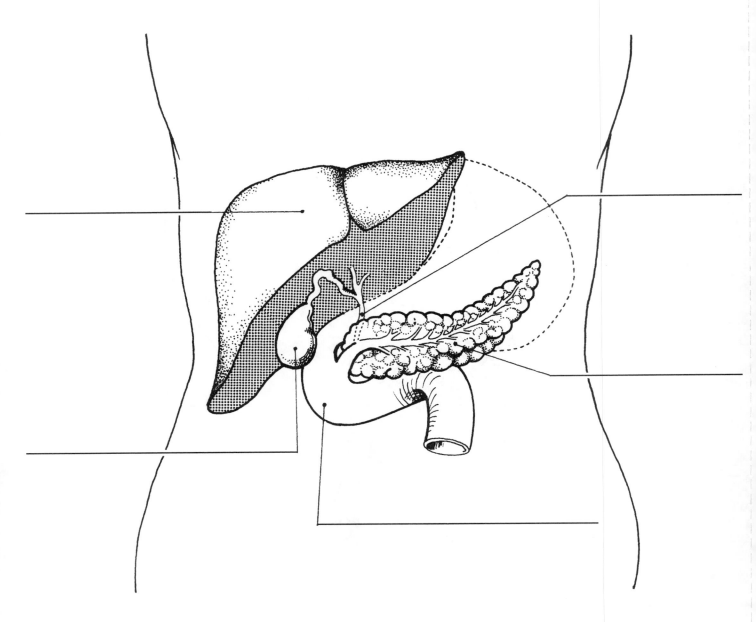

bile duct	duodenum	gallbladder
liver	pancreas	

Inside the Mouth

Label the parts of the mouth.

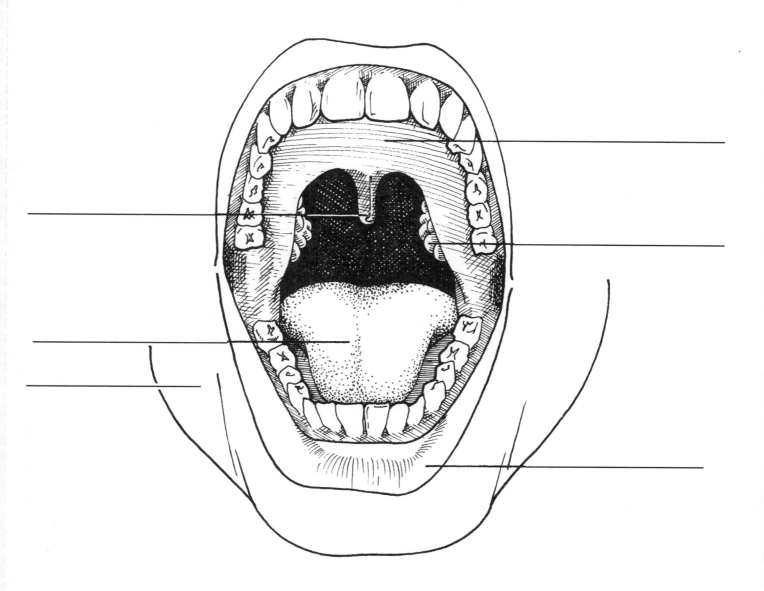

| cheek | lip | palate |
| tongue | tonsils | uvula |

The Alimentary Canal

Label each part of the digestive system and draw a line to match the description to the part of the digestive system.

entrance to food tube; chews food

stores food for 3–4 hours while digestion occurs; churning breaks down proteins

opening for waste exit

20-foot-long tube for final digestion

muscular tube that squeezes food down to the stomach

stores solid waste; removes water

first part of small intestine; food enters it from the stomach

makes chemicals to break down food

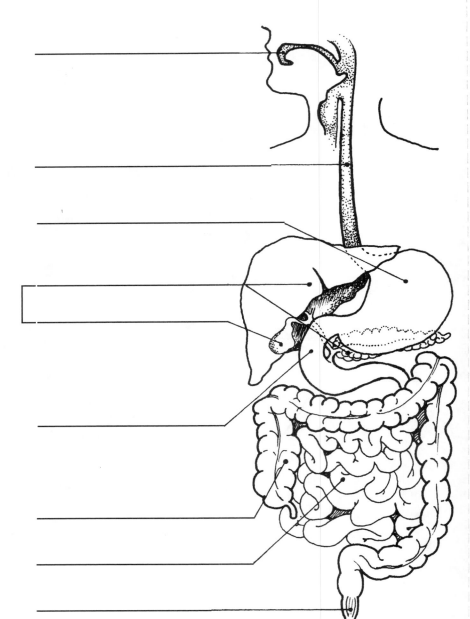

anus	duodenum	esophagus
gallbladder	large intestine	liver, pancreas
mouth	small intestine	stomach

Digestive System Crossword

Use the word bank to complete the puzzle.

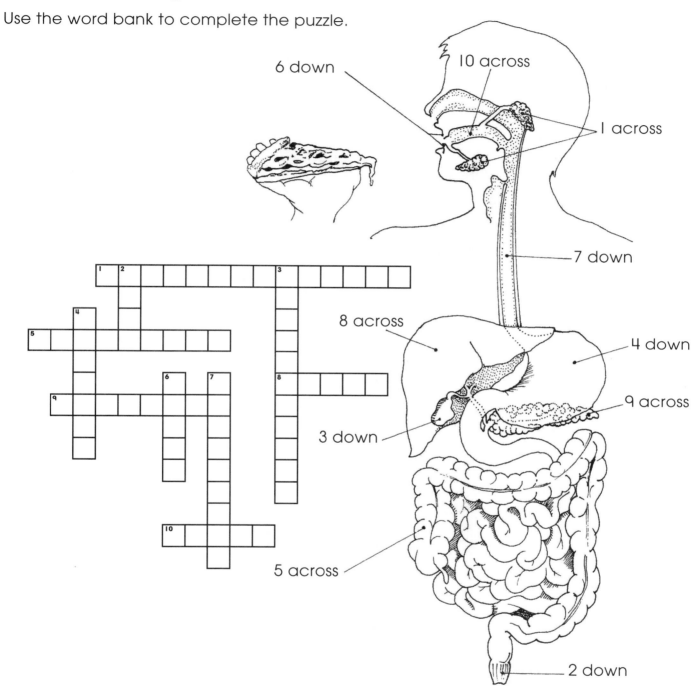

6 down

10 across

1 across

7 down

8 across

4 down

3 down

9 across

5 across

2 down

anus	esophagus	gallbladder	intestine
liver	mouth	pancreas	salivary glands
stomach	teeth		

The Urinary System

Label the parts of the urinary system.

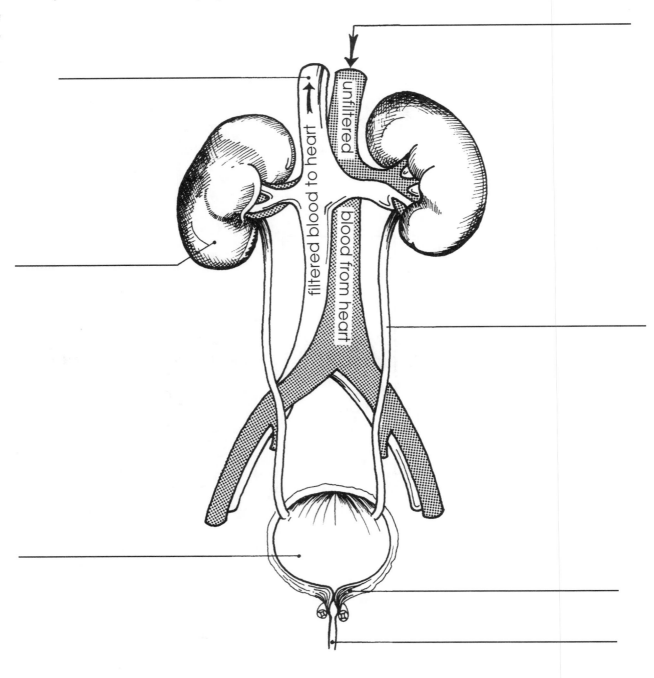

artery	bladder	kidney
muscle	ureter	urethra
vein		

Waste Removal

The important job of removing bodily wastes is performed by the skin and the organs of the urinary and respiratory systems.

Label the excretory organs. Then, complete the chart by checking the boxes to show the function(s) of each organ.

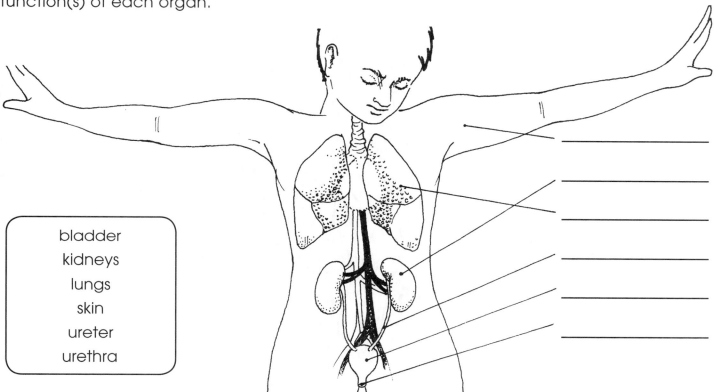

bladder
kidneys
lungs
skin
ureter
urethra

Function	Excretory Organs			
	kidneys	lungs	skin	bladder
removes water				
brings oxygen to blood				
removes salt				
stores urine				
removes carbon dioxide				
produces urine				
removes body heat				

The Central Nervous System

Label the parts of the central nervous system.

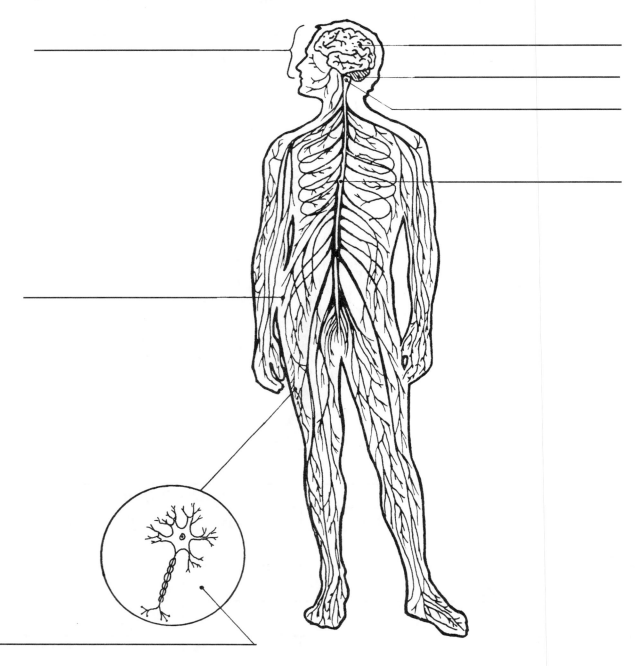

brain	brain stem	cerebellum
cerebrum	nerve cell	nerve
spinal cord		

Neurons

Label the parts of a neuron.

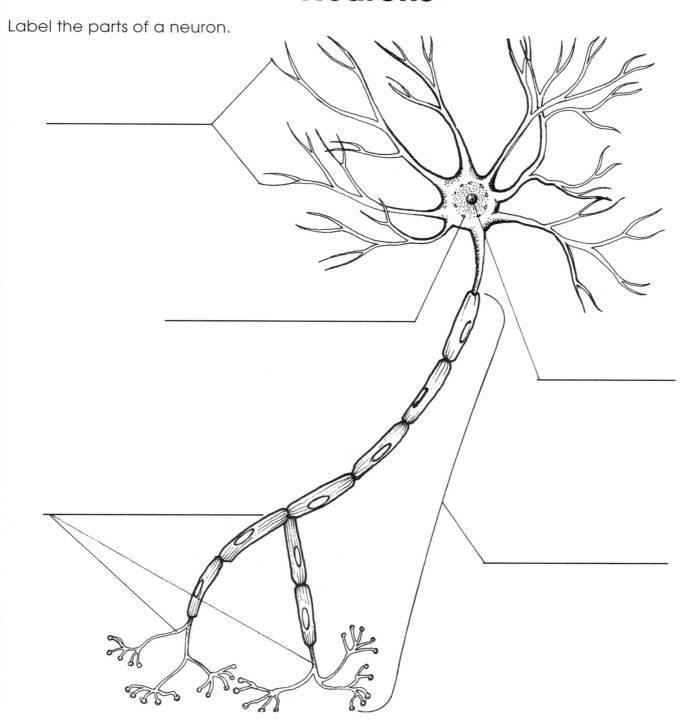

| axon | cell body | dendrites |
| nucleus | axon terminals | |

Transmitters of Impulses

Neurons act as "go-betweens" in the sending and receiving of impulses within the nervous system. The diagrams illustrate how impulses pass from one neuron to another.

Label the parts of the diagram.

Synapse

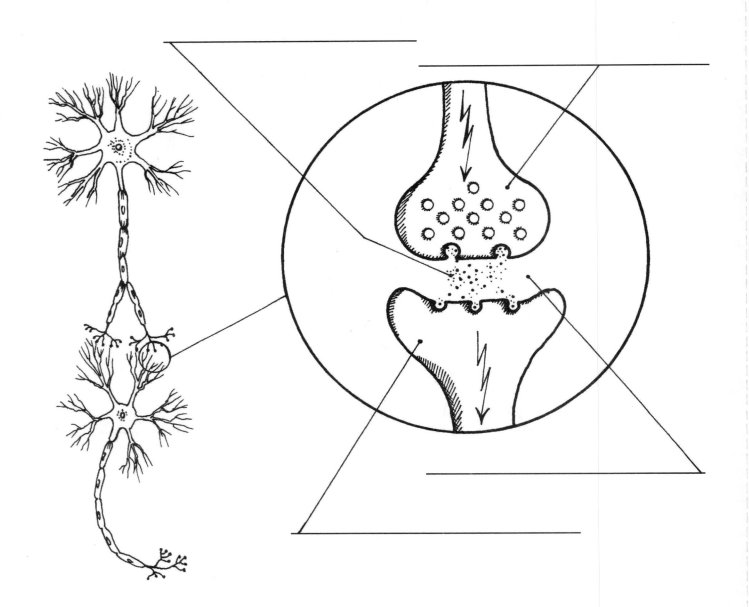

| axon terminal | dendrite |
| synaptic cleft | transmitting molecule |

The Brain

Label the parts of the brain.

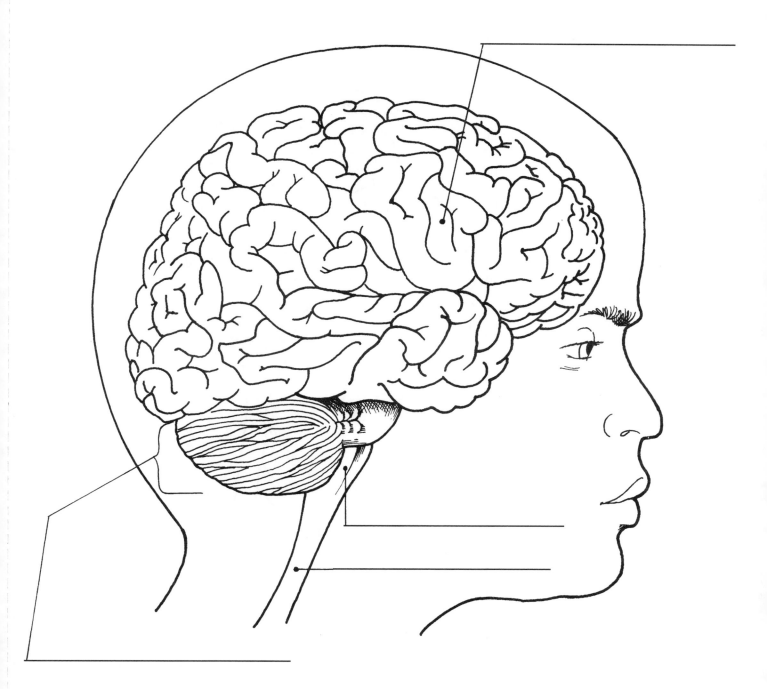

brain stem	cerebellum	cerebrum
spinal cord		

The Nervous System

Two of the nervous systems in the human body are the **central** and the **peripheral**.

Label these two systems and their parts.

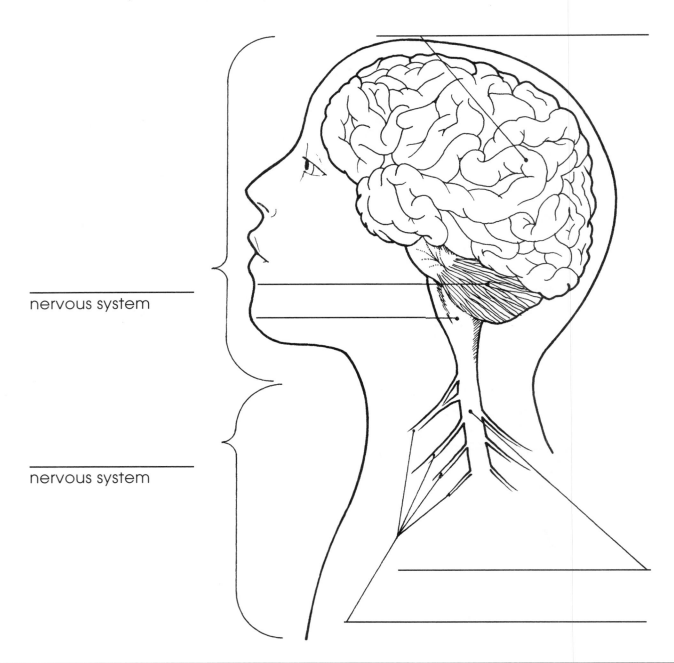

_____
nervous system

_____
nervous system

| central | cerebellum | cerebrum | medulla |
| peripheral | spinal cord | spinal nerves | |

The Nervous System at Work

Write the letter of each function next to its matching part. Then, draw a line from the pictured part of the nervous system to its function.

Part

1. cerebrum _____   4. spinal cord _____

2. cerebellum _____   5. spinal nerves _____

3. medulla _____

Functions

a. It controls balance and muscular coordination.

b. It controls thought, voluntary movement, memory and learning, and also processes information from the senses.

c. They carry impulses between the spinal cord and body parts.

d. It controls breathing, heartbeat, and other vital body processes.

e. It relays impulses between the brain and other parts of the body.

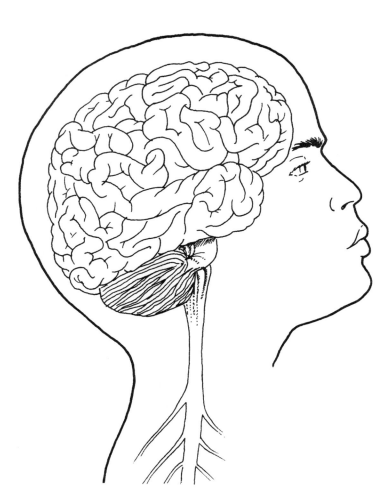

Nervous System Functions

Label the parts of the nervous system.

a. _____

b. _____

c. _____

d. _____

e. _____

cerebellum
cerebrum
medulla
spinal cord
spinal nerves

Complete the chart by writing the name of each nervous system part and its function.

Nervous System	
Part	**Function**
a.	
b.	
c.	
d.	
e.	

Name_____

The Autonomic Nervous System

The **autonomic nervous system** works almost independently of the central nervous system. It controls the life-sustaining functions of the body such as breathing, digestion, and heartbeat. These organs and muscle tissues work involuntarily.

Label the parts of the autonomic nervous system.

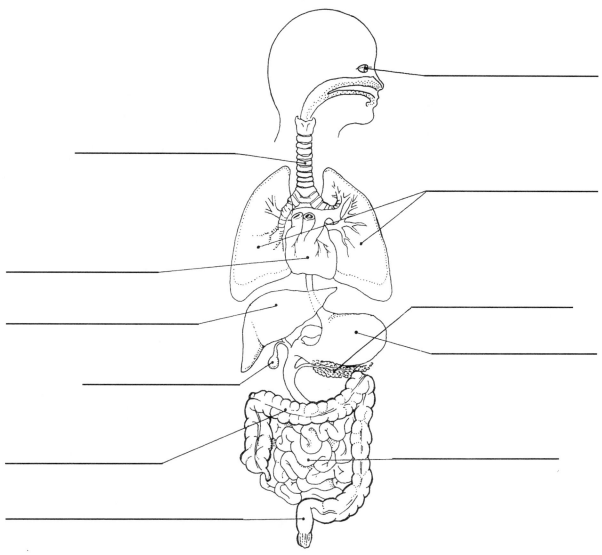

eye	gallbladder	heart
large intestine	liver	lungs
pancreas	rectum	small intestine
stomach	trachea	

Nervous System Crossword

Use the word bank to complete the puzzle.

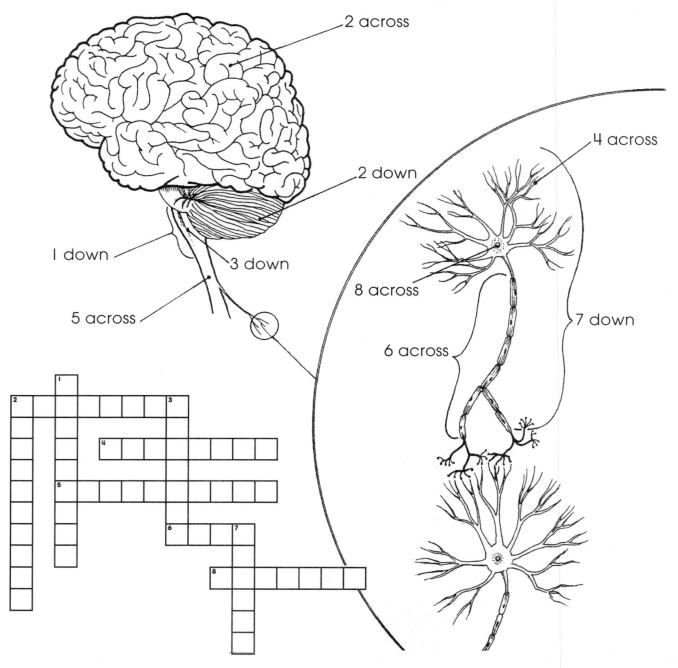

axon	brain stem	cerebellum
cerebrum	dendrite	medulla
neuron	nucleus	spinal cord

The Endocrine System

The endocrine glands help control many of the body's functions. Label the glands of the endocrine system.

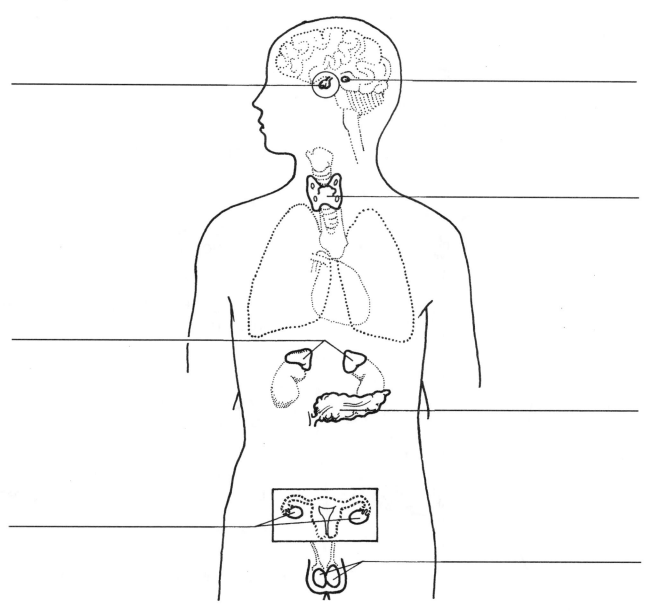

adrenal glands	ovaries (female)
pancreas	pineal gland
pituitary gland	testes (male)
thyroid gland	

Glands

Draw a line from the name of the gland to its picture and from the picture of the gland to its function.

Gland   **Function**

thyroid •

pituitary •   • Controls other glands and body growth

parathyroids •   • Control the amount of calcium in your blood

                                               • Controls the rate that food is turned into energy

adrenal •   • Helps the body's immune system to recognize and reject germs

thymus •   • Affects kidneys and reacts when the body is excited, angry, or frightened

ovaries •   • Controls the body's use of glucose

pancreas •   • Produce female characteristics and initiate female bodily functions

Endocrine Glands

Label the glands in the endocrine system.

a. _____

b. _____

c. _____

d. _____

e. _____

f. _____

g. _____

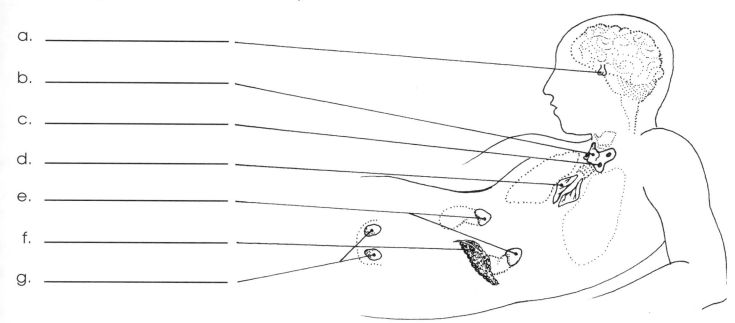

Complete the chart by writing the name of each gland and its function.

Gland	Function
a.	
b.	
c.	
d.	
e.	
f.	
g.	

adrenals	pancreas	parathyroid	pituitary
testes	thymus	thyroid	

The Sensory Systems

The brain gets information from outside the body through many different sense organs. Label the different sense organs and the nerve cell pictured on this page.

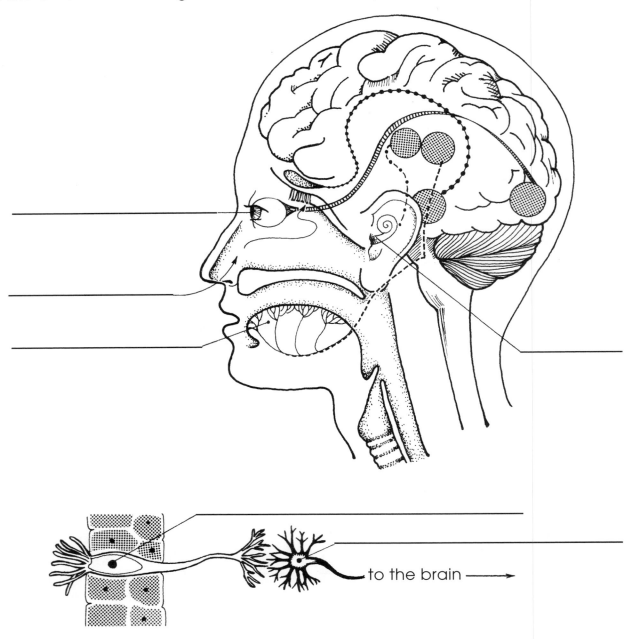

to the brain ⟶

ear	eye
nose	receptor nerve cell
sensory nerve cell	tongue

Taste

The tongue can sense four basic tastes—sweet, sour, bitter, and salty. Label the different sense areas of the tongue and the different parts of this sense organ.

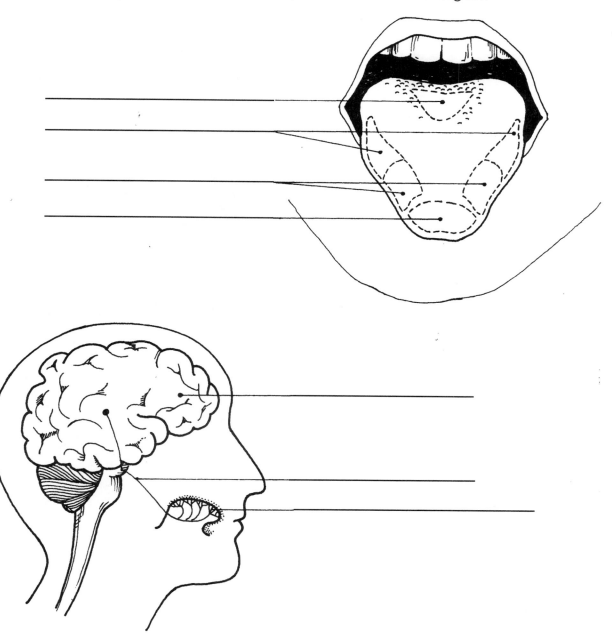

brain	bitter	nerve
salty	sour	sweet
taste bud		

The Nose

Label the parts of the nose.

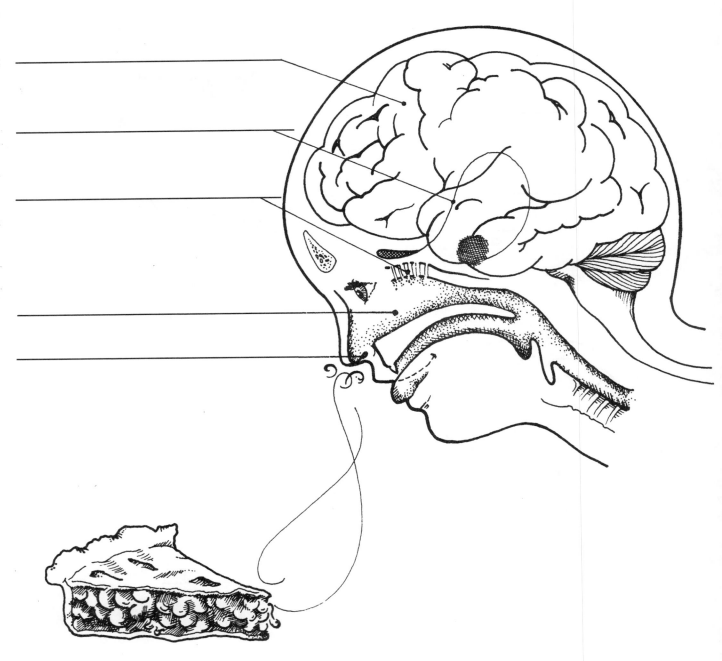

brain	nasal passage	nostril
olfactory nerve	receptor cells	

The Ear

Label the parts of the ear.

anvil	auditory canal	auditory nerve
auricle (pinna)	cochlea	eardrum
eustachian tube	hammer	oval window
semicircular canals	stirrup	wax gland

The Outer Ear

Label the three major regions of the ear. Then, label the parts of the outer ear.

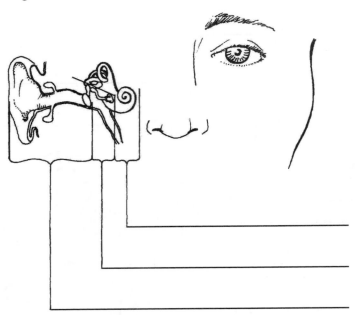

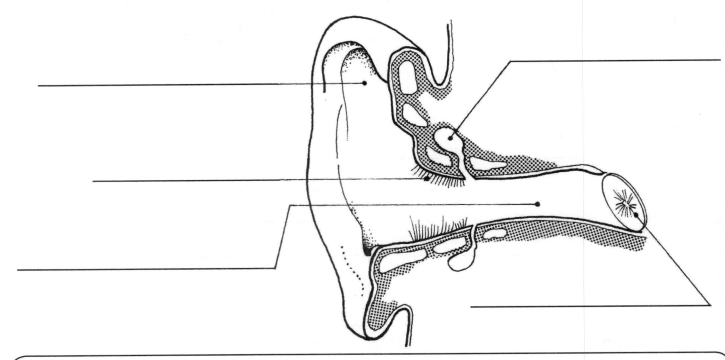

auditory canal	auricle (pinna)	eardrum
hairs	inner ear	middle ear
outer ear	wax gland	

The Middle Ear

Label the three major regions of the ear. Then, label the parts of the middle ear.

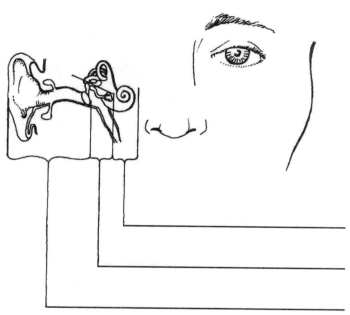

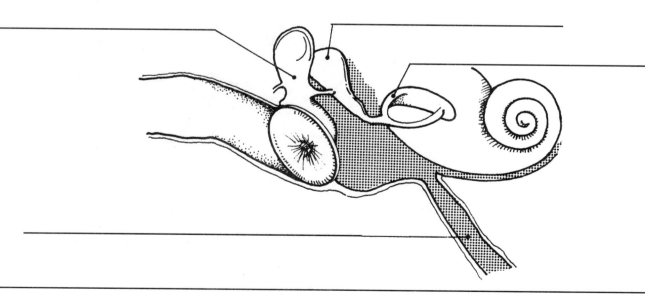

anvil	eustachian tube	hammer
inner ear	middle ear	outer ear
stirrup		

The Inner Ear

Label the three major regions of the ear. Then, label the parts of the inner ear.

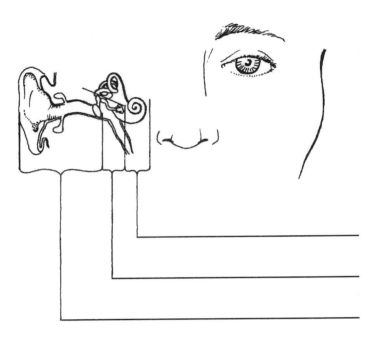

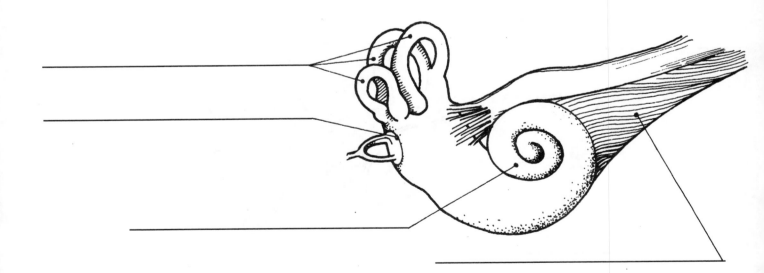

auditory nerve   cochlea   inner ear

middle ear   outer ear   oval window

semicircular canals

Ear, Nose, and Throat

The ears, nose, mouth, and throat are all connected to each other. Label the parts in the diagram.

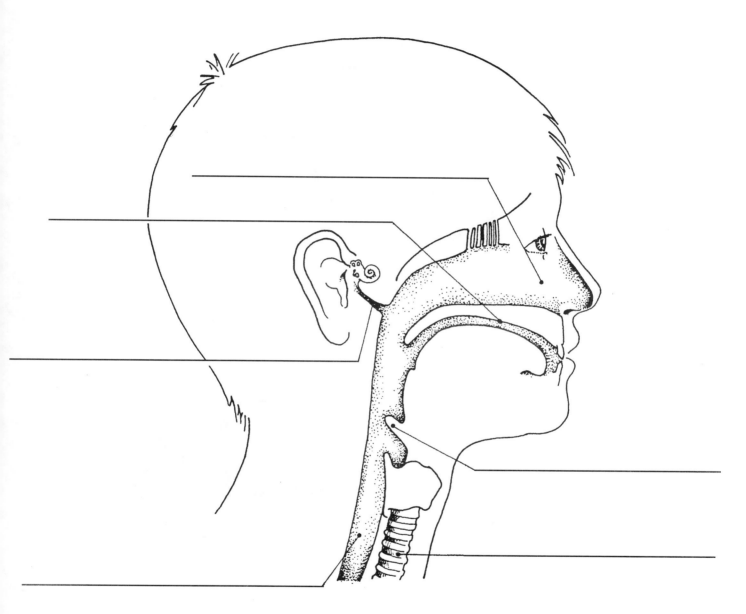

| epiglottis | esophagus | eustachian tube |
| nasal passage | roof of the mouth | windpipe (trachea) |

The Eye

Label the parts of the eye. Some words may be used more than once.

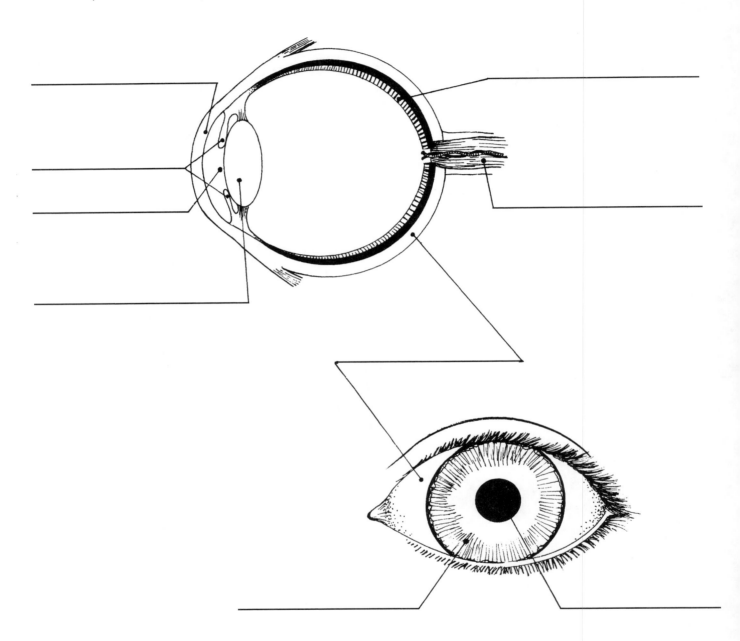

cornea	iris	lens
optic nerve	pupil	retina
sclera		

Name_____

Inside the Eye

Label the parts of the eye.

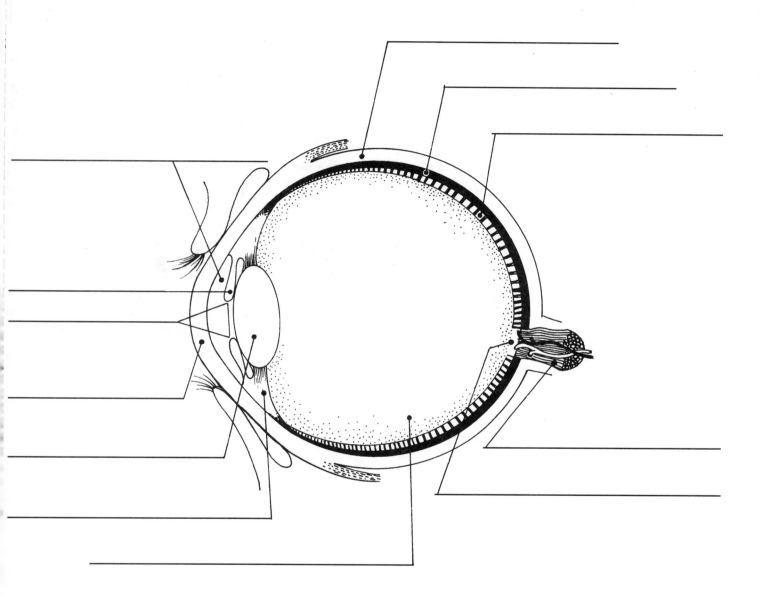

aqueous humor (watery fluid)	blind spot	choroid
ciliary muscles (lens-controlling muscles)	cornea	iris
lens	optic nerve	pupil
retina	sclera	vitreous humor (clear jelly)

Eye-to-Brain Connection

Your eyes gather the rays of light coming off of an object. They change the light rays into nerve impulses, but your brain interprets these impulses and "draws" a picture of the image.

Label the parts of this "eye-to-brain connection."

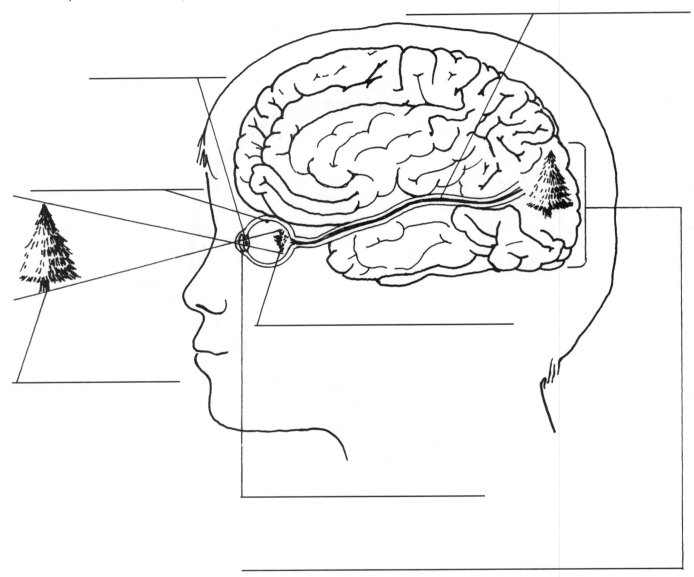

cornea	image	lens
optic nerve	retina	upside-down image
visual cortex		

Eye Protection

The eyeball is very well protected. Label the parts of the eye and those that help protect it.

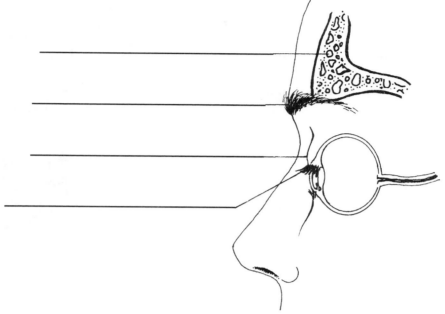

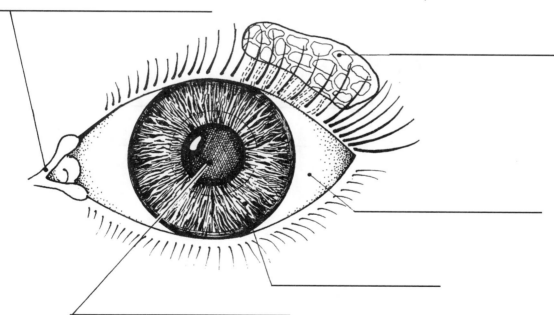

eyebrow	eyelash	eyelid
iris	pupil	sclera
skull	tear duct	tear (lacrimal) gland

The Eye and the Camera

A camera is very similar to the eye. Label the parts of the eye and the camera. Then, write the job of each part. Some words may be used more than once.

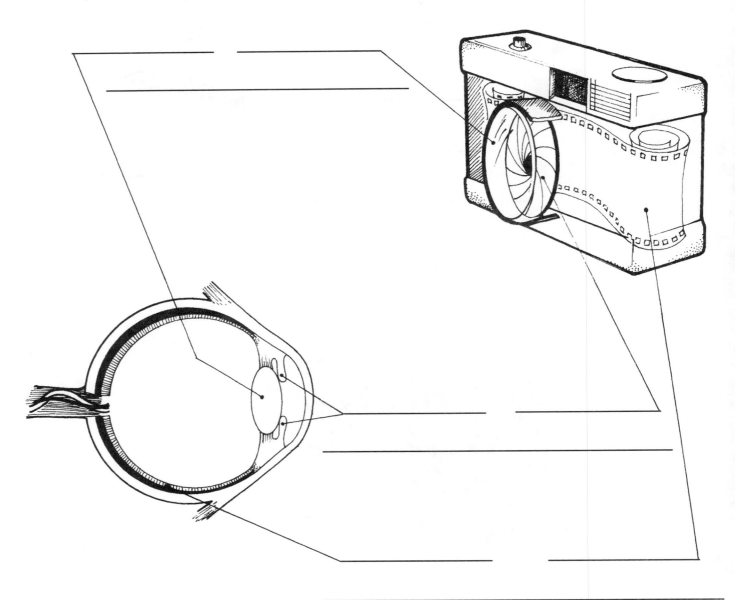

Jobs	Parts	
adjusts the amount of light	film	iris
light-sensitive material	lens	retina
used to focus		

Eyesight

Eyes can vary in shape. This can give people problems with their sight.

Label each eye.

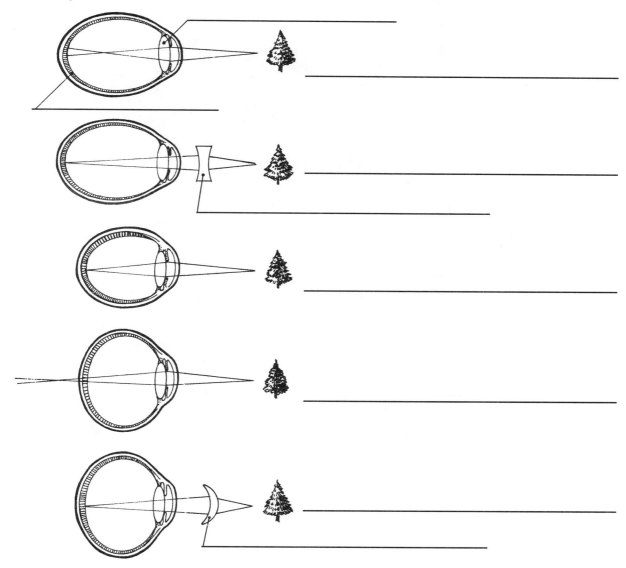

_____

_____

_____

_____

_____

_____

_____

concave lens	convex lens
corrected farsighted vision	corrected nearsighted vision
farsighted vision	lens
nearsighted vision	normal vision
retina	

Ear and Eye Crossword

Use the word bank to complete the puzzle.

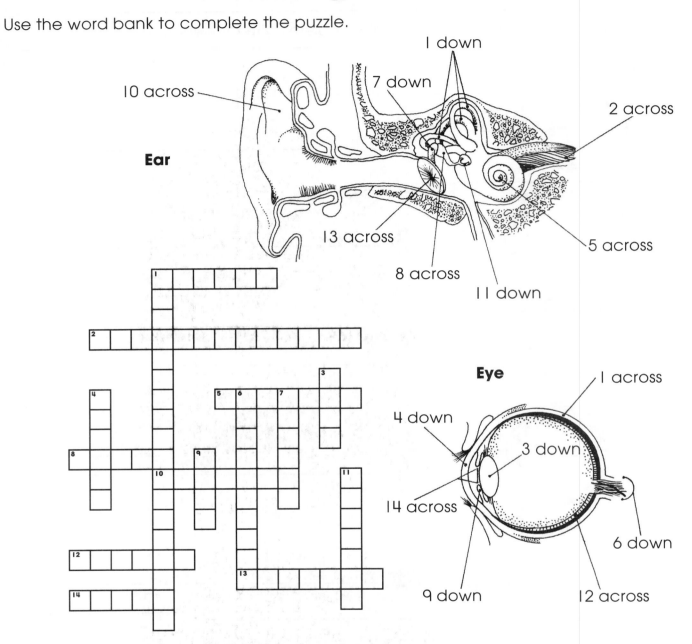

10 across

Ear

1 down

7 down

2 across

13 across

8 across

11 down

5 across

Eye

1 across

4 down

3 down

14 across

9 down

6 down

12 across

anvil	auditory nerve	auricle
cochlea	cornea	eardrum
hammer	iris	lens
optic nerve	pupil	retina
sclera	semicircular canals	stirrup

Skin Layers

The skin is made up of many layers. These layers contain hair, nerves, blood vessels, and glands.

Label the diagram.

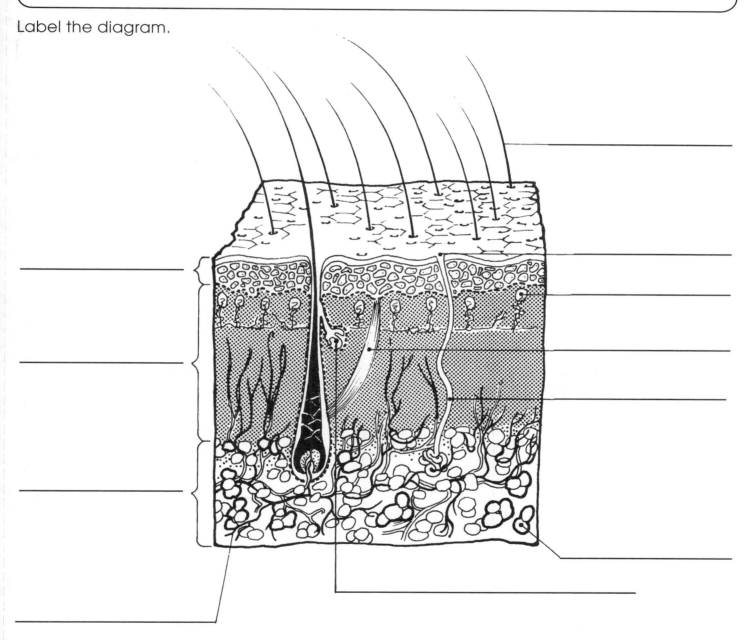

blood vessel	dermis	epidermis	fat cell
fat layer (hypodermis)	hair	hair muscle	nerve
oil gland	pore	sweat gland	

How a Pimple Develops

Pimples begin to form when **sebum**, an oily substance given off by the sebaceous gland, gets trapped beneath the surface of the skin.

Number the three stages of pimple formation. Then, label the parts illustrated in each stage.

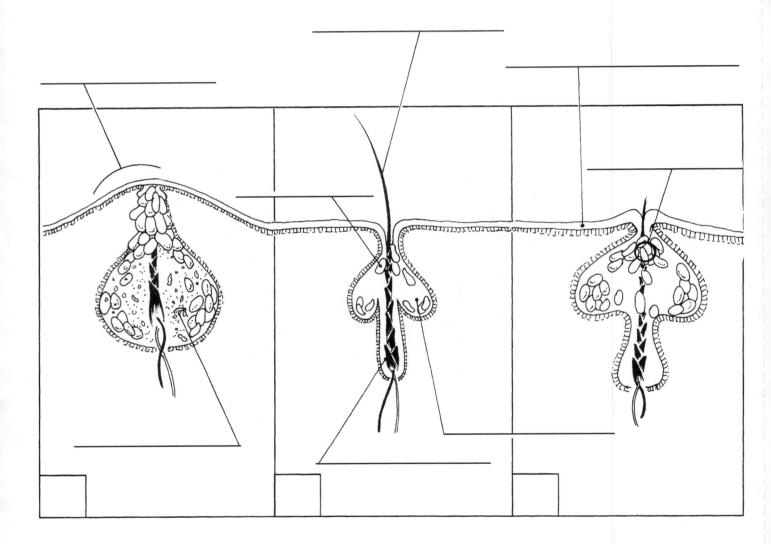

blockage	epidermis	hair	hair follicle
pimple	pus	sebaceous gland	sebum

Temperature Regulation

On cold days, the skin has a way to keep in the body's warmth. On hot days, the skin can cool the body.

Label the pictures **warm day** or **cool day.** Then, label the parts of the skin.

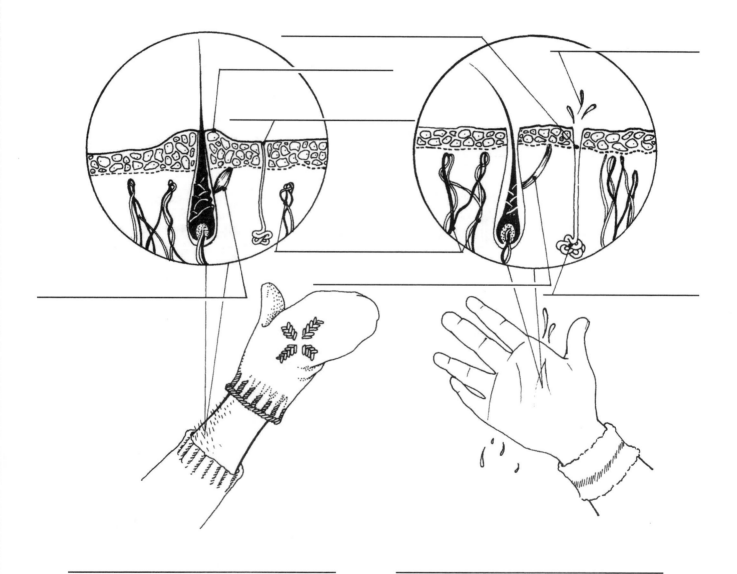

blood vessels	closed sweat pore
contracted muscle	goose bump
open sweat pore	relaxed muscle
sweat	sweat gland

Body Tissues

Many of the body's organs are made of a variety of tissues working together. There are four kinds of tissue: **connective**, **epithelial**, **muscle**, and **nerve**. Each has a specialized function.

Study the pictures and read the descriptions. Write the name of each tissue beneath its description and label the tissue parts in each picture.

Composed of relatively few cells and surrounded by larger amounts of nonliving material; supports and connects other tissues

_____

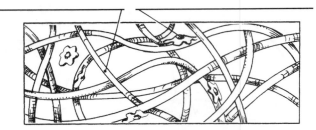

Made up of cells that can contract and relax; allows the body to make internal and external movements

_____

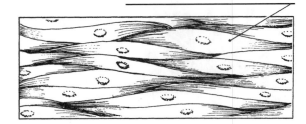

Specialized cells which carry electrical signals between the brain and other parts of the body

_____

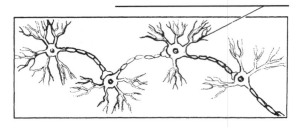

Tightly packed cells forming a covering for the skin and lining the hollow internal organs

_____

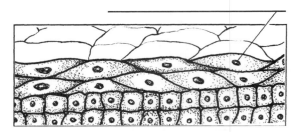

cell	cell nucleus	collagen
connective tissue	epithelial tissue	fibroblast
muscle tissue	nerve fiber	nerve tissue

Fingerprints

The ridges in fingertips form unique patterns. No two people have the same pattern, not even identical twins. The ridges on fingers form three main groups of patterns—the **arch**, the **loop**, and the **whorl**.

arch

loop

whorl

Make a record of your own fingerprints on the chart.

1. Place the side of your fingertip on an inkpad and roll your finger from one side to the other.

2. Place the side of each inked finger on the chart and roll it softly to leave a clear, crisp print.

3. Label each print using the examples as a guide.

Right Hand

Thumb	Index	Middle	Ring	Little

Left Hand

Thumb	Index	Middle	Ring	Little

Toenails and Fingernails

Nails are a specialized part of your skin that protect the ends of your toes and fingers.

Label the parts of the nails. Words may be used more than once.

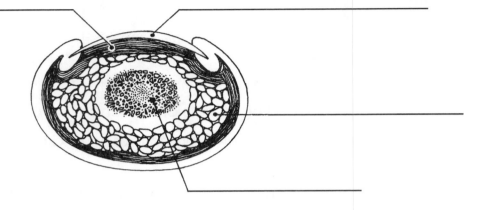

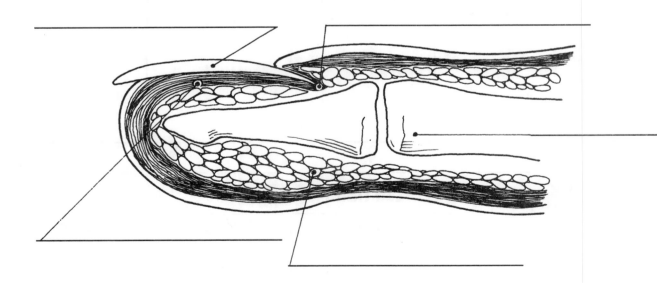

bone	fatty tissue	nail bed
nail plate	nail root	

Reproductive System—Male

The purpose of the reproductive system is to create new life. Label the parts of the male reproductive system.

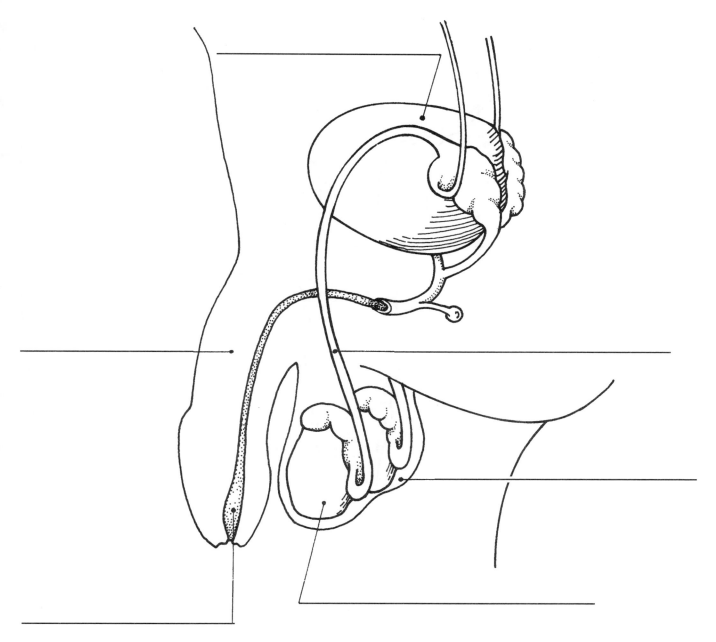

bladder	penis	scrotum
sperm tube	testis	urethra

Reproductive System—Female

The purpose of the reproductive system is to create new life. Label the parts of the female reproductive system.

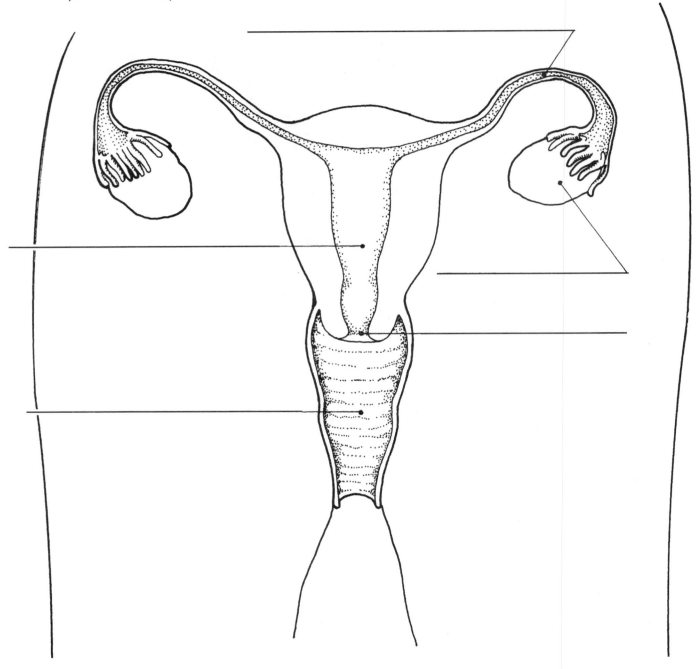

cervix	Fallopian tube	ovary
uterus	vagina	

New Life

From the time of conception, a single cell divides and keeps dividing until it forms the six trillion cells of a human newborn baby. This development takes nine months.

Write the matching description of a baby's development under each picture.

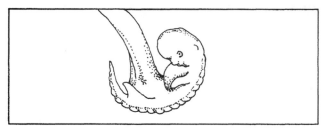

4 weeks _____

_____

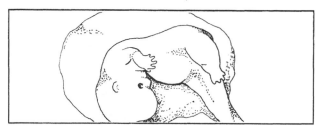

8 weeks _____

_____

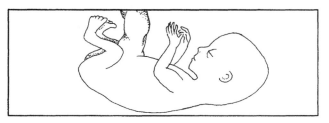

3 months _____

_____

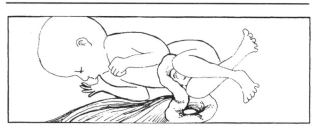

4–6 months _____

_____

7 months _____

_____

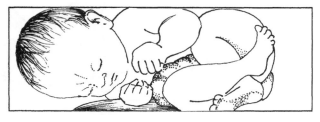

9 months _____

_____

can survive birth with special care

develops tiny arm and leg buds; heart begins to beat

ears, eyes, nose, fingers, and toes are formed

first movements felt; heartbeat can be monitored with a stethoscope

fully developed with organs that can function on their own

has recognizable human features; sex can be determined

Birth of a Baby

When a baby is fully developed within the uterus, a hormone in the pituitary gland stimulates the muscles of the uterus. These muscle contractions signal the beginning of labor. The opening to the uterus, the cervix, gradually enlarges to allow the baby to pass through. The amniotic sac that surrounds the baby will break, releasing a gush of amniotic fluid. After the baby is born, the placenta separates from the wall of the uterus and is pushed out by more muscle contractions.

Label the diagram of the birth of a baby.

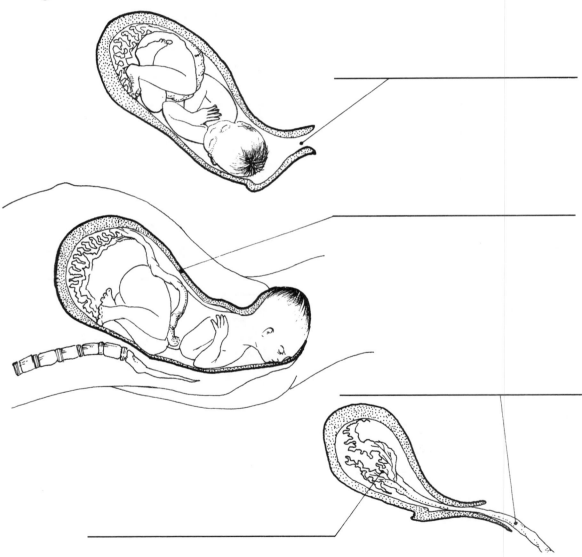

| birth canal | placenta | umbilical cord | uterus |

Genes

There are more than 40,000 **genes** that determine which traits each person has. These traits, such as dark hair or blue eyes, are inherited from parents. There are two strengths of traits: **dominant** is the strongest and **recessive** is the weakest.

Place checks in each chart to show which parent(s) would have the dominant or recessive genes in each category if the child had the dominant or recessive trait. Circle the traits you have inherited.

D = Dominant Trait   R = Recessive Trait

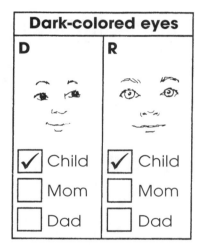

Dark-colored eyes

D	R
☑ Child	☑ Child
☐ Mom	☐ Mom
☐ Dad	☐ Dad

Blond hair

D	R
☑ Child	☑ Child
☐ Mom	☐ Mom
☐ Dad	☐ Dad

Dimples

D	R
☑ Child	☑ Child
☐ Mom	☐ Mom
☐ Dad	☐ Dad

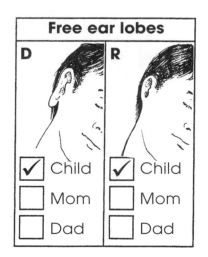

Free ear lobes

D	R
☑ Child	☑ Child
☐ Mom	☐ Mom
☐ Dad	☐ Dad

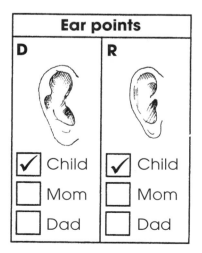

Ear points

D	R
☑ Child	☑ Child
☐ Mom	☐ Mom
☐ Dad	☐ Dad

Genes (con't.)

D = Dominant Trait   R = Recessive Trait

Can roll tongue

D | **R**

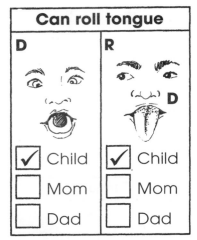

☑ Child   ☑ Child
☐ Mom   ☐ Mom
☐ Dad   ☐ Dad

Can fold tongue

D | **R**

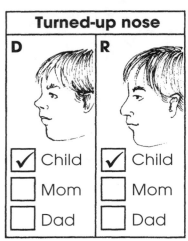

☑ Child   ☑ Child
☐ Mom   ☐ Mom
☐ Dad   ☐ Dad

Clockwise hair whorl

D | **R**

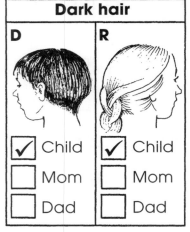

☑ Child   ☑ Child
☐ Mom   ☐ Mom
☐ Dad   ☐ Dad

Widow's peak

D | **R**

☑ Child   ☑ Child
☐ Mom   ☐ Mom
☐ Dad   ☐ Dad

Turned-up nose

D | **R**

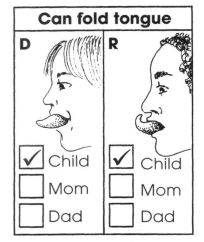

☑ Child   ☑ Child
☐ Mom   ☐ Mom
☐ Dad   ☐ Dad

Dark hair

D | **R**

☑ Child   ☑ Child
☐ Mom   ☐ Mom
☐ Dad   ☐ Dad

Freckles

D | **R**

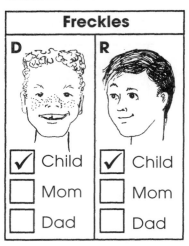

☑ Child   ☑ Child
☐ Mom   ☐ Mom
☐ Dad   ☐ Dad

Hair on middle of fingers

D | **R**

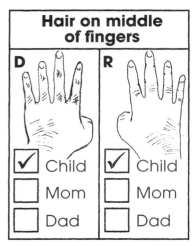

☑ Child   ☑ Child
☐ Mom   ☐ Mom
☐ Dad   ☐ Dad

Bent little finger

D | **R**

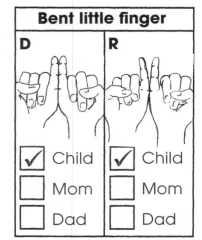

☑ Child   ☑ Child
☐ Mom   ☐ Mom
☐ Dad   ☐ Dad

Inside the Head (Page A)

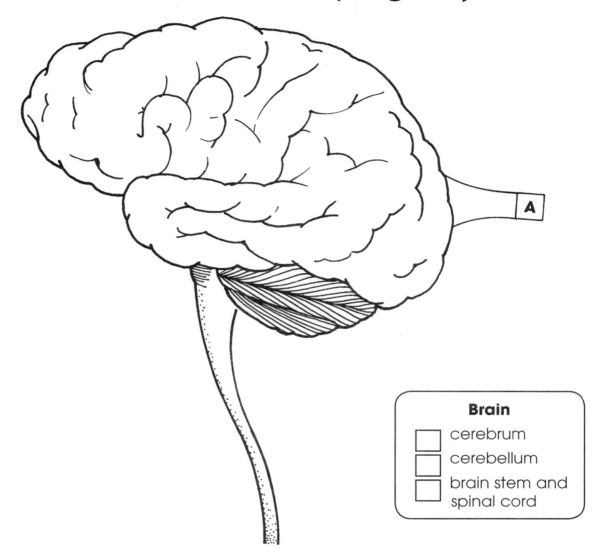

Brain
☐ cerebrum
☐ cerebellum
☐ brain stem and spinal cord

1. Color the keys on pages A, B, and C. Then, use the keys to color the corresponding parts.

2. Cut out the head parts and keys on pages A, B, and C.

3. Glue the head parts and the keys onto the head outline on page D, attaching them to the page by the tabs only.

4. Overlap the different head parts on the head outline. Notice the locations of the various head parts.

Inside the Head (Page B)

Breathing
- ☐ nasal passage
- ☐ windpipe
- ☐ voice box
- ☐ esophagus
- ☐ tongue
- ☐ epiglottis
- ☐ palate

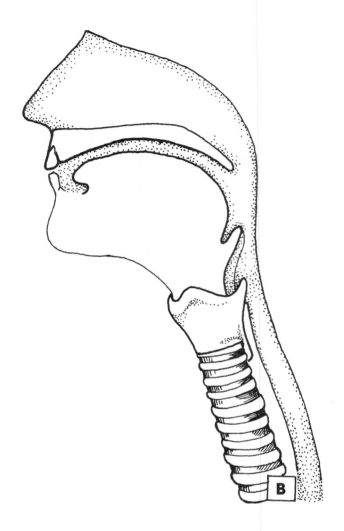

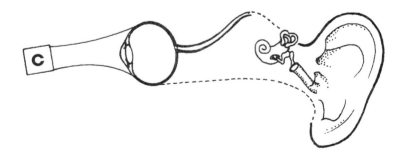

Eyes and Ears
- ☐ eye
- ☐ optic nerve
- ☐ outer ear
- ☐ inner ear
- ☐ eardrum

Inside the Head (Page C)

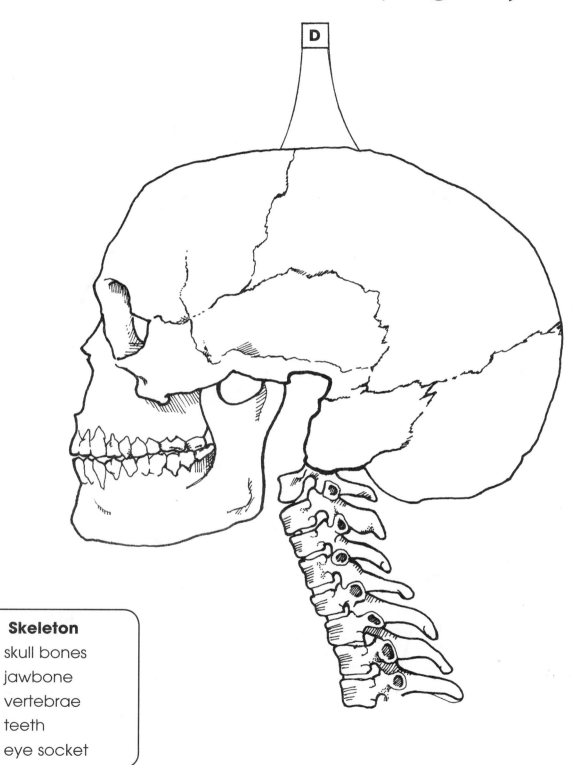

Skeleton

- [ ] skull bones
- [ ] jawbone
- [ ] vertebrae
- [ ] teeth
- [ ] eye socket

Inside the Head (Page D)

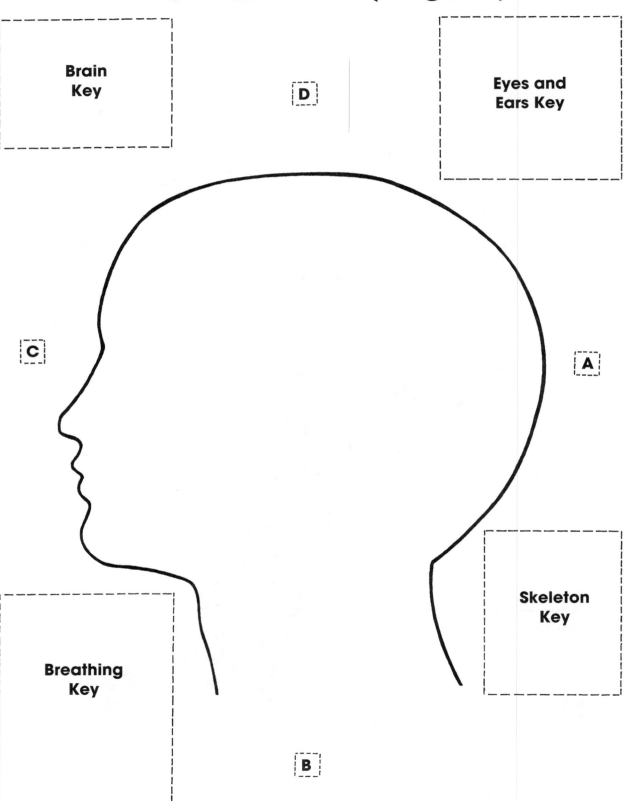

Brain
Key

D

Eyes and
Ears Key

C

A

Breathing
Key

Skeleton
Key

B

Body Systems (Page A)

Glue pages A and B together by overlapping the stars of page A over the stars of page B.

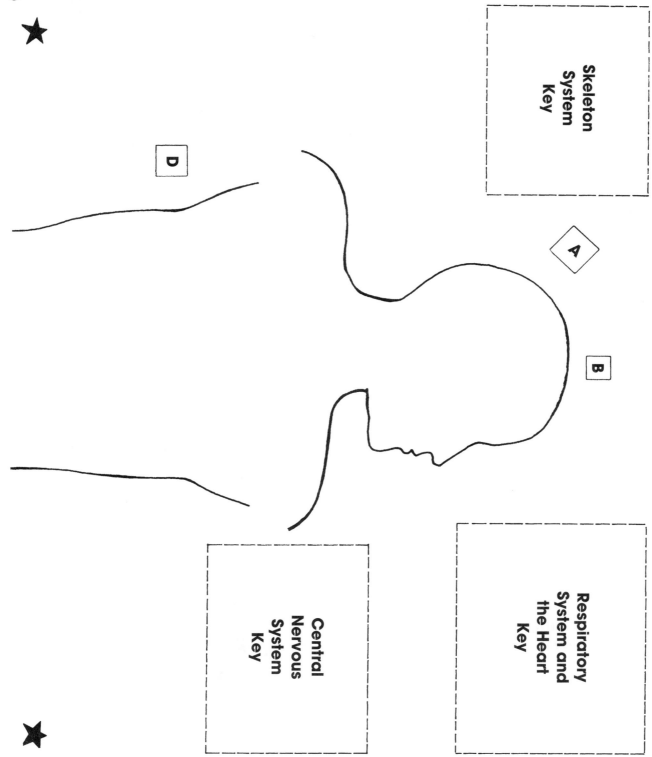

Body Systems (Page B)

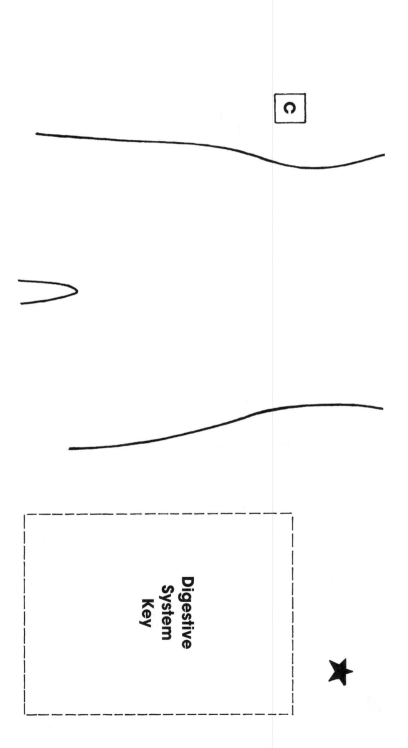

Body Systems (Page C)

On pages C, D, and E are pictures of four body systems. Next to each body system is a key that lists the parts of the system.

1. Color each of the parts of a body system a different color.

2. Color the boxes in the key to match the parts of the system.

3. Cut out the body systems and keys on pages C, D, and E.

4. Glue the tabs only of each body system on the spaces that are marked on pages A and B.

5. Glue the keys in the spaces that are marked on pages A and B.

Overlap the different body systems to see where each system is located in your body.

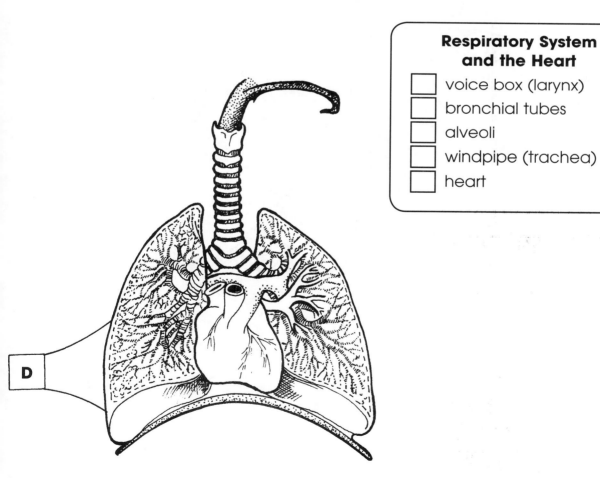

**Respiratory System
and the Heart**

☐ voice box (larynx)
☐ bronchial tubes
☐ alveoli
☐ windpipe (trachea)
☐ heart

Body Systems (Page D)

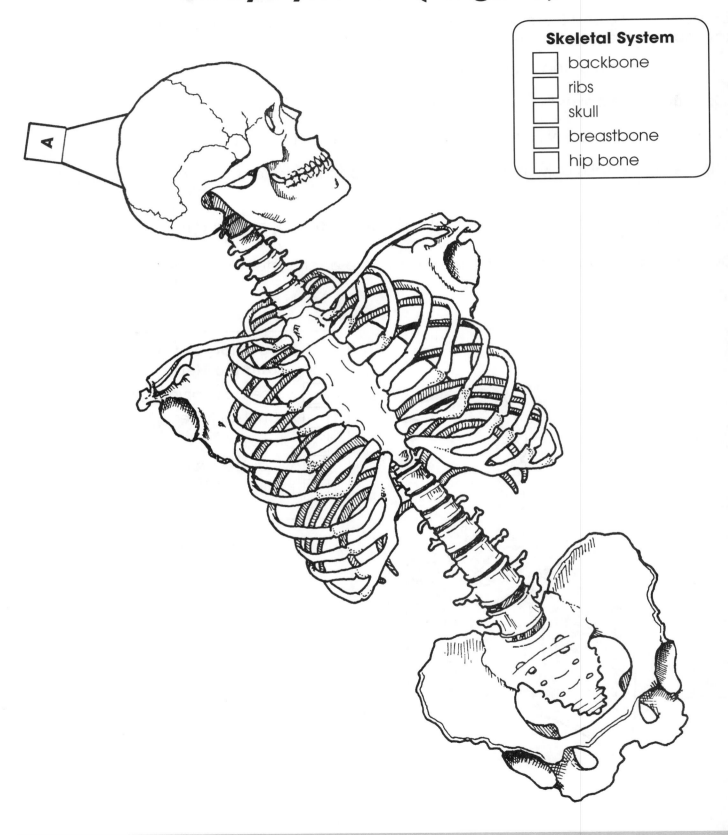

Body Systems (Page E)

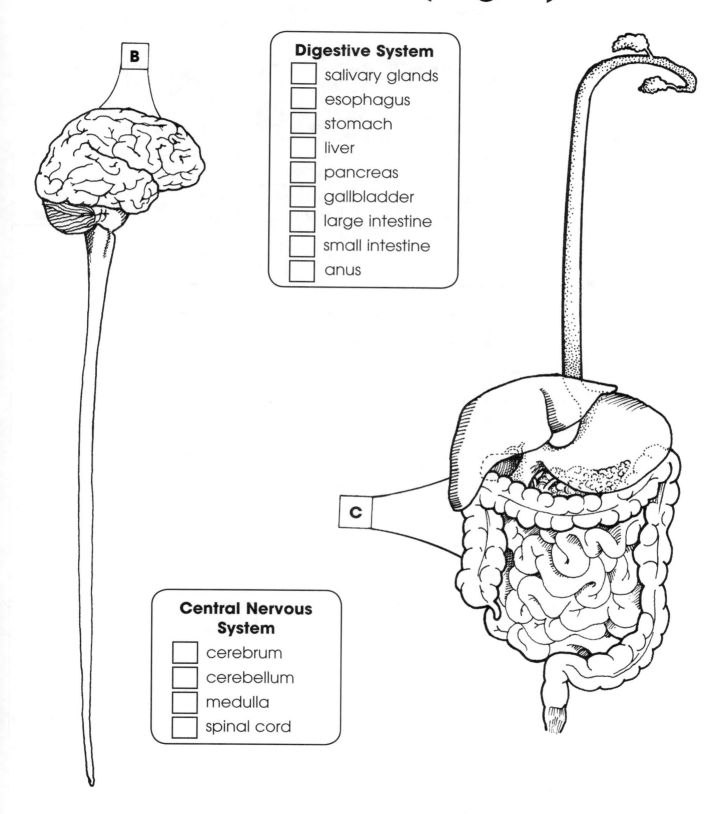

B

Digestive System
- [ ] salivary glands
- [ ] esophagus
- [ ] stomach
- [ ] liver
- [ ] pancreas
- [ ] gallbladder
- [ ] large intestine
- [ ] small intestine
- [ ] anus

C

Central Nervous System
- [ ] cerebrum
- [ ] cerebellum
- [ ] medulla
- [ ] spinal cord

Organ Systems

Place an **X** in the boxes that show to which system or systems each organ belongs.

Organs	Systems						
	Diges-tive	**Respi-ratory**	**Urinary**	**Repro-ductive**	**Circu-latory**	**Nervous**	**Endo-crine**
bladder							
brain							
heart							
ovaries							
liver							
pancreas							
kidneys							
spinal cord							
lungs							
small intestine							
diaphragm							
mouth							
nerves							
testes							
thyroid gland							
arteries							
esophagus							
cerebellum							

Human Body Crossword

Use the word bank to complete the puzzle.

Across

1. Outer layer of skin
4. The blood pump
6. Stores urine
10. The "bite" is the _____ of the teeth.
11. Opening to the uterus
12. Structure and bone system
13. The inside of the hand
14. Controls body growth and other glands
17. A break in a bone
20. Created by the rhythm of the heart
21. Female sex glands
22. Determine human traits

Down

1. Waste removal system
2. Outer layer of the tooth
3. Upper arm bone
5. Gland activated by excitement, anger, or fright
7. _____ fluid surrounds a fetus.
8. Long food tube
9. Joint found in elbow
12. Oily substance given off by the sebaceous gland
13. Gland which controls the body's use of glucose
15. Place where arteries are close to skin; place to take pulse
16. Muscles are attached to the skeleton by _____.
18. Male sex glands
19. Framework of bones that supports the lower part of the abdomen

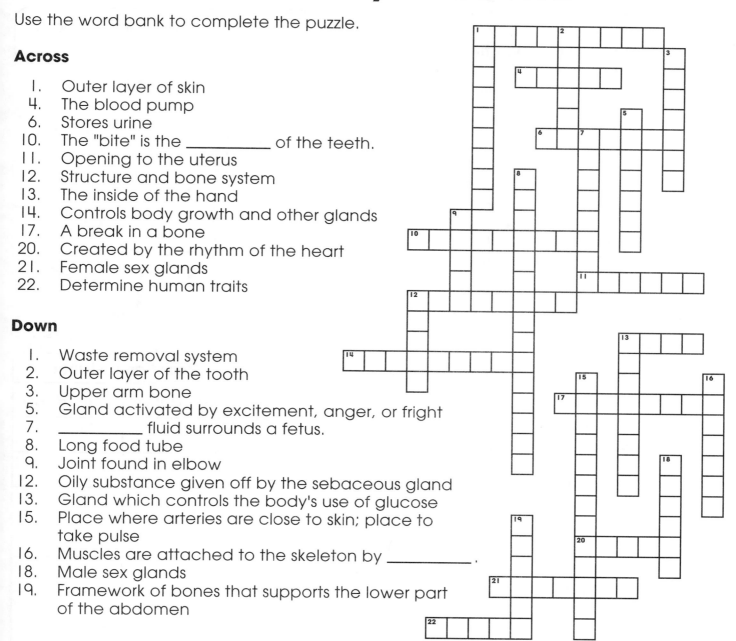

adrenal	alignment	alimentary canal	amniotic	bladder
cervix	enamel	epidermis	excretory	fracture
genes	heart	hinge	humerus	ovaries
palm	pancreas	pelvis	pituitary	pressure point
pulse	sebum	skeleton	tendons	testes

Experiment: Reaction Time

The time it takes for your sensory organs to send a message to your brain and your body to respond is called **reaction time**.

This experiment tests reaction time. Follow the directions.

Materials: 30cm metric ruler

Procedure:

1. Place your left arm on a table with your hand over the edge.

2. Space your thumb and index fingers about 4 cm apart.

3. Have a partner hold the ruler by the 30cm end, with the other end just above your open thumb and index finger.

4. Your partner will say "go" and drop the ruler.

5. Catch the ruler with your thumb and index finger as quickly as possible.

6. Check the distance fallen by taking a reading at the bottom of the index finger.

7. Record your results.

8. Repeat the procedure 10 times with each hand.

    Are you right-handed or left-handed? Which of your hands was the quickest?

    _____

    Did others find the same results?

    _____

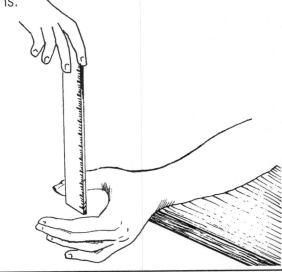

Trial	Reaction Distance	
	Left Hand	Right Hand
1.		
2.		
3.		
4.		
5.		
6.		
7.		
8.		
9.		
10.		

Experiment: Heart Rate

When the heart pumps, it forces blood out into the arteries. The walls of the arteries expand and contract to the rhythm of the heart, which creates a **pulse**.

You can feel your pulse where the arteries are close to the surface of the skin. Two good places to feel a pulse are on the inside of the wrist and on the neck to the side of the windpipe.

The type of activity you are doing can greatly affect the rate of your pulse. Try the experiments below. Complete the chart by counting the number of heart beats in 15 seconds and multiplying that number by 4 to get the pulse rate for 1 minute.

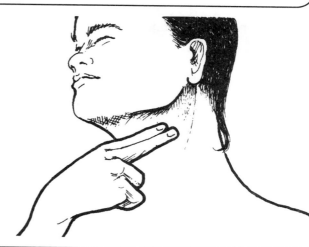

Activity	Pulse rate for 15 seconds	Pulse rate per minute	How pulse was affected
Sitting still for 10 minutes			
Running in place for 3 minutes			
Just after finishing your lunch or dinner			
While sitting in bed in the morning			
Just after getting ready for school			

Caution: Exercise activities may require adult supervision. Before beginning any exercise activity, ask families' permission. You should always warm up prior to beginning any exercise activity and should stop immediately if you feel any discomfort during exercise.

Proper Portions

This graphic represents the portions recommended by the US Department of Agriculture.

Find Out

What foods do you eat each day? Choose a day and make a chart of what you eat. Record the kind of food and the number of servings.

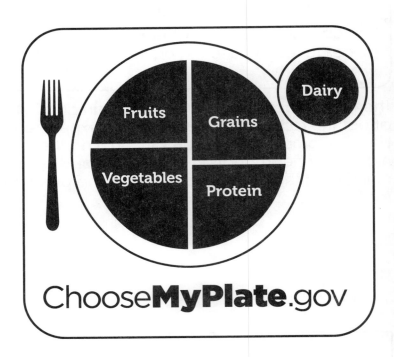

Group	Breakfast	Lunch	Dinner	Snack
grains				
vegetables				
fruits				
protein				
dairy				
fats, oils, sweets				

How did you do? Compare your servings to the recommended proportions.

Name_____

Snacks and Nutrition

Some snack foods are better for you than others. Foods that contain smaller amounts of fat are usually much better for you.

Labels might not use the name **sugar** when they list sweeteners. Watch for other names for sugar, such as dextrose, lactose, corn syrup, fructose, molasses, and sucrose.

Snacker's Survey

Write the food group to which each snack belongs. Then, using a scale of 1–10, with 1 being the lowest, give each snack a taste score and a nutrition score.

Snack	Food Group	Taste Score	Nutrition Score
apple			
cheese			
cookie			
potato chips			
orange			
carrot			
cake			
candy bar			
bagel			
beef jerky			
popcorn			
pretzels			

Nutrients

The body is made up of millions of cells that need food to stay alive. The body needs **nutrients** from foods to help the cells grow and repair themselves. Nutrients are divided into six major groups: **fats**, **proteins**, **carbohydrates**, **minerals**, **vitamins**, and **water**.

Read each clue. Identify the nutrient.

1. "I'm the body's building material. I make new tissue. There is plenty of me in milk, beans, meat, and peanuts."

   Who am I? _____

2. "I have energy for work and play. Find me in starchy foods such as pasta and potatoes."

   Who am I? _____

3. "I help build strong bones and teeth. I am important for healthy red blood. Find me in all four food groups."

   Who am I? _____

4. "I am a concentrated source of energy. Find me in oily and greasy foods, such as bacon, salad dressing, and butter. I also help maintain healthy skin and hair."

   Who am I? _____

5. "I am one of the essential nutrients. I don't give any energy, but I do help the body get energy from the other nutrients."

   Who am I? _____

6. "I make up over half of human body weight. My job is to carry all of the good nutrients throughout the body. I also help the body to remove wastes."

   Who am I? _____

Word Bank

carbohydrate

fat

mineral

protein

vitamin

water

Nutrition Facts

Looking closely at the information on a cereal box provides interesting facts about the product.

Carefully read the nutrition facts shown for the cereal Corn Balls. Answer the questions. Compare these answers with the information found on a box of cereal you might eat for breakfast.

	Corn Balls	Your Cereal
What kind of grain is used?		
Is sugar used?		
What position is sugar on the list of ingredients?		
List other sweeteners.		
How many calories are present per serving without milk?		
How many calories are present per serving when eaten with 1/2 cup of skim milk?		
How much protein is present per serving?		
How many vitamins and minerals does the cereal contain?		
How much cholesterol is in one serving?		
How much fat is in one serving?		
How much carbohydrate is in one serving?		

Nutrition Facts

Serving Size: 1 cup (55g)
Servings Per Package: About 12

Amount Per Serving	Cereal	Cereal With 1/2 Cup Skim Milk
Calories from Fat	210	250
Calories	10	10

		%Daily Value**
Total Fat 1g*	**2%**	**2%**
Saturated Fat 0g	**0%**	**0%**
Trans Fat 0g		
Polyunsaturated Fat 0.5g		
Monounsaturated Fat 0g		
Cholesterol 0mg	**0%**	**1%**
Sodium 10mg	**0%**	**3%**
Potassium 180mg	**5%**	**11%**
Total Carbohydrate 45g	**15%**	**17%**
Dietary Fiber 6g	**24%**	**24%**
Soluble Fiber 1g		
Insoluble Fiber 5g		
Sugars 11g		
Other Carbohydrates 28g		
Protein 5g		

Calcium	2%	15%
Iron	10%	10%
Vitamin D	0%	10%
Thiamin	10%	10%
Riboflavin	4%	15%
Niacin	15%	15%
Vitamin B6	8%	10%
Folate (Folic Acid)	4%	6%
Vitamin B12	2%	10%
Phosphorus	15%	25%
Magnesium	10%	15%
Zinc	10%	15%
Copper	10%	10%

Not a significant source of Vitamin A and Vitamin C.

* Amount in cereal. One-half cup skim milk contributes an additional 65mg sodium, 6g total carbohydrate (6g sugars) and 4g protein.

** Percent Daily Values are based on a 2,000 calorie diet. Your daily values may be higher or lower depending on your calorie needs.

	Calories	2,000	2,500
Total Fat	Less than	65g	80g
Saturated Fat	Less than	20g	25g
Cholesterol	Less than	300mg	300mg
Sodium	Less than	2,400mg	2,400mg
Potassium		3,500mg	3,500mg
Total Carbohydrate		300g	375g
Dietary Fiber		25g	30g

Calories per gram: Fat 9 • Carbohydrate 4 • Protein 4

Ingredients: Corn, sugar, corn syrup, molasses, salt, annatto color.

Burning Calories

Regular exercise strengthens the heart and helps burn calories to maintain a healthy weight.

The activities named below list the number of calories burned by a 150-pound person when he or she engages in an activity for 30 minutes. Circle the seven activities below that burn the most calories.

Activity	Calories Burned in 30 Minutes	Activity	Calories Burned in 30 Minutes
cross country skiing	210	homework	55
running (7 mph)	275	raquetball	365
shuffleboard	90	baseball	60
bicycling (stationary)	150	soccer	360
aerobic dancing	200	swimming	265
watching TV	45	tennis	225
walking (5.5 mph)	190	basketball	345

Complete the chart below to keep a record of the exercise you do for one week.

	Type of Exercise(s)	Length of Time (Minutes)	Approximate Calories Burned
Sunday			
Monday			
Tuesday			
Wednesday			
Thursday			
Friday			
Saturday			

Medicine Labels

The labels on medicine containers give important information. Labels should always be read carefully.

Read the information on the cough medicine labels below. Answer the questions.

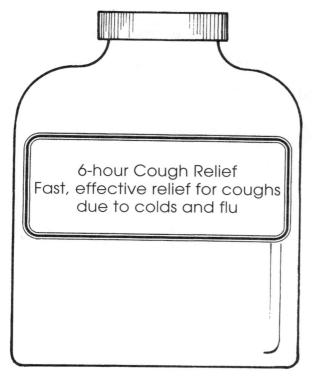

6-hour Cough Relief
Fast, effective relief for coughs due to colds and flu

Recommended Dosage
Children (5–12 years): 1 teaspoon every 6 hours
Adults: 2 teaspoons every 6 hours
Caution: *Do not administer to children under 5. No more than 4 dosages per day. This product may cause drowsiness; use caution if operating machinery or driving a vehicle. Should not be taken if you are pregnant or nursing a child.*

If cough or fever persists, consult a physician.
Exp. Date: 8/2020

1. What is the adult dosage? _____

2. What is a child's dosage? _____

3. What is a side effect of this medicine? _____

4. Who should not take this medicine? _____

5. How many dosages per day can be taken safely? _____

6. What is the expiration date of this medicine? _____

7. What action should be taken if the medicine does not relieve your cough?

    _____

8. For what symptoms should this medicine be taken?

    _____

Poisons

Children can be very curious. They love to touch things and pick them up. Very young children like to put things into their mouths. What action should be taken if a child swallows a poisonous material?

Read the following safety procedures.

CALL YOUR POISON CONTROL CENTER, HOSPITAL, PHYSICIAN, OR EMERGENCY PHONE NUMBER IMMEDIATELY!

If you cannot obtain emergency advice, follow these procedures.

• If the poison is **corrosive** (paint remover, household cleaners, gasoline, drain opener, ammonia, or lye), **DO NOT** make the patient vomit. Give the patient water or milk to dilute the poison.

• If the poison is **not corrosive** (insect spray, aspirin, pesticides, or medicine), **make the patient vomit** or use a poison control kit. To force the patient to vomit, touch the back of his or her throat.

Place a **V** on each picture that shows poison that should be vomited if swallowed. Circle each poison that should not be vomited if swallowed.

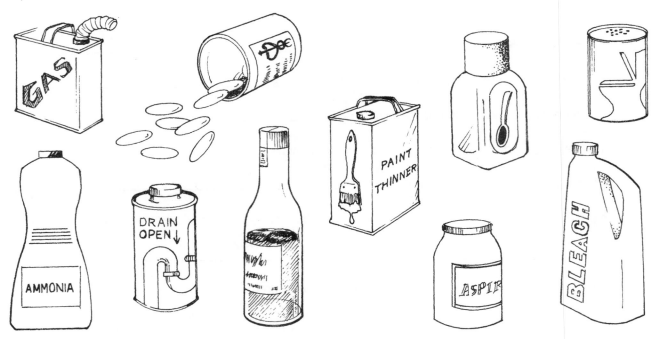

Answer Key

The Body Systems

The human body is made of many systems that work together in groups. Label the different body systems in each group.

Movement group   Control group

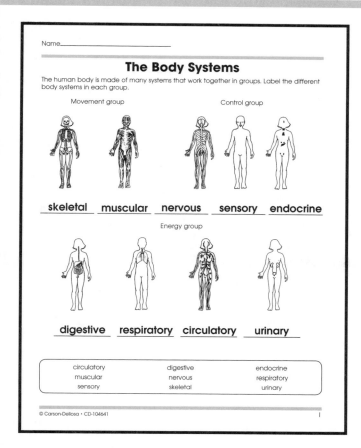

skeletal   muscular   nervous   sensory   endocrine

Energy group

digestive   respiratory   circulatory   urinary

circulatory	digestive	endocrine
muscular	nervous	respiratory
sensory	skeletal	urinary

© Carson-Dellosa • CD-104641   1

Name_____

Body Parts

Label the parts of the body.

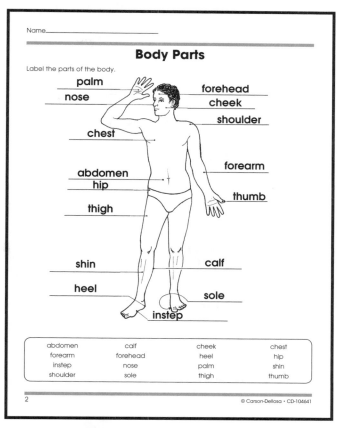

palm
nose
forehead
cheek
shoulder
chest
forearm
abdomen
hip
thumb
thigh
shin
calf
heel
sole
instep

abdomen	calf	cheek	chest
forearm	forehead	heel	hip
instep	nose	palm	shin
shoulder	sole	thigh	thumb

2   © Carson-Dellosa • CD-104641

Name_____

The Skeletal System

Label the skeleton with the common and scientific names of each bone.

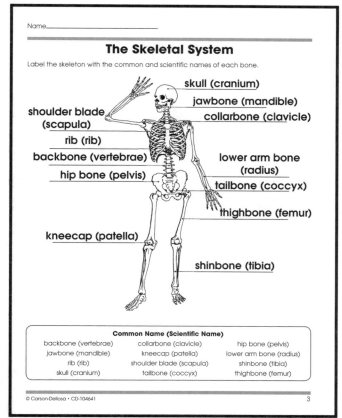

skull (cranium)
jawbone (mandible)
collarbone (clavicle)
shoulder blade (scapula)
rib (rib)
backbone (vertebrae)
lower arm bone (radius)
hip bone (pelvis)
tailbone (coccyx)
thighbone (femur)
kneecap (patella)
shinbone (tibia)

Common Name (Scientific Name)

backbone (vertebrae)	collarbone (clavicle)	hip bone (pelvis)
jawbone (mandible)	kneecap (patella)	lower arm bone (radius)
rib (rib)	shoulder blade (scapula)	shinbone (tibia)
skull (cranium)	tailbone (coccyx)	thighbone (femur)

© Carson-Dellosa • CD-104641   3

Name_____

Head Bones

Label the bones that are found in the head and neck.

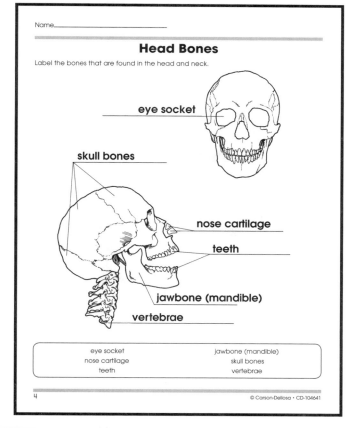

eye socket
skull bones
nose cartilage
teeth
jawbone (mandible)
vertebrae

eye socket	jawbone (mandible)
nose cartilage	skull bones
teeth	vertebrae

4   © Carson-Dellosa • CD-104641

Answer Key

Name_____

Kinds of Joints

The place where two or more bones meet is called a **joint**. Joints are either movable or immovable. There are four kinds of movable joints: **hinge**, **pivot**, **gliding**, and **ball-and-socket**.

Label the three kinds of joints shown. List examples of where each kind of joint is found.

Kind of Joint	Joint	Man-Made Equal	Example
ball-and-socket			hip shoulder
hinge			knee elbow
gliding		(no man-made equal)	spine wrist

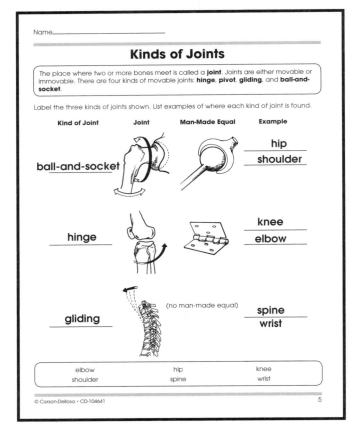

elbow	hip	knee
shoulder	spine	wrist

5

Name_____

Joints in the Body

Label each type of joint on the skeleton. Some words may be used more than once.

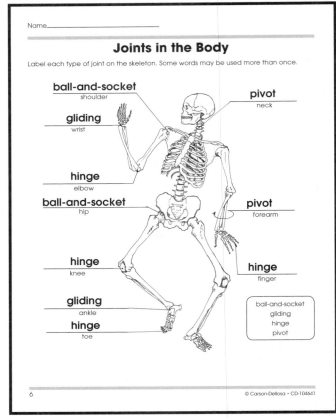

ball-and-socket — shoulder
pivot — neck
gliding — wrist
hinge — elbow
ball-and-socket — hip
pivot — forearm
hinge — knee
hinge — finger
gliding — ankle
hinge — toe

ball-and-socket
gliding
hinge
pivot

6

Name_____

Bones

Label the parts of the long bone in the diagram.

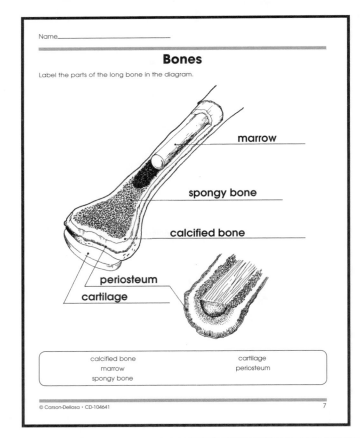

marrow

spongy bone

calcified bone

periosteum

cartilage

calcified bone	cartilage
marrow	periosteum
spongy bone	

7

Name_____

Breaks in Bones

A break in a bone is called a **fracture**. Some of the common types of fractures are pictured.

Label the different kinds of fractures.

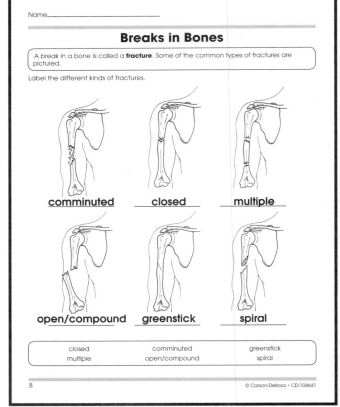

comminuted   closed   multiple

open/compound   greenstick   spiral

closed	comminuted	greenstick
multiple	open/compound	spiral

8

Answer Key

Name_____

The Backbone

Label the regions of the spine, or vertebral column.

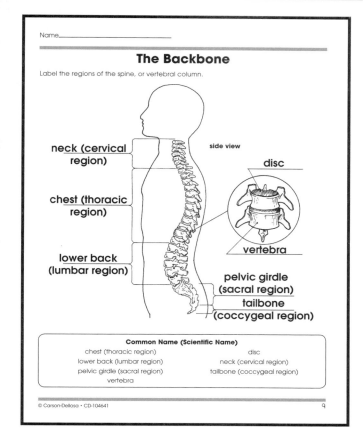

side view

neck (cervical region)

disc

chest (thoracic region)

lower back (lumbar region)

vertebra

pelvic girdle (sacral region)

tailbone (coccygeal region)

Common Name (Scientific Name)	
chest (thoracic region)	disc
lower back (lumbar region)	neck (cervical region)
pelvic girdle (sacral region)	tailbone (coccygeal region)
vertebra	

Name_____

The Hands and Feet

Label the bones of the hand and foot. Some words may be used more than once.

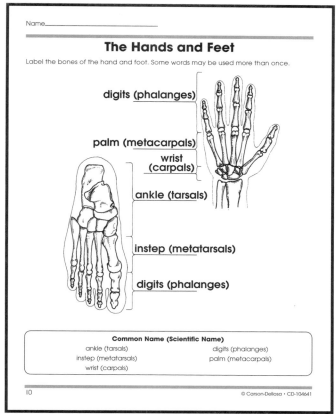

digits (phalanges)

palm (metacarpals)

wrist (carpals)

ankle (tarsals)

instep (metatarsals)

digits (phalanges)

Common Name (Scientific Name)	
ankle (tarsals)	digits (phalanges)
instep (metatarsals)	palm (metacarpals)
wrist (carpals)	

Name_____

Leg Bones

Label the different leg bones and regions.

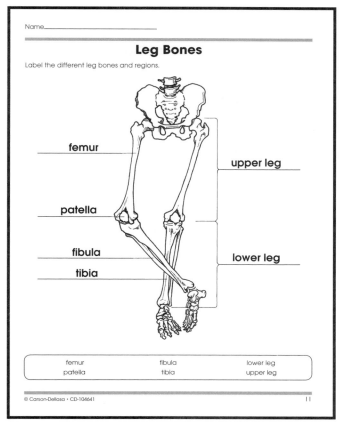

femur

upper leg

patella

fibula

lower leg

tibia

femur	fibula	lower leg
patella	tibia	upper leg

Name_____

The Pelvis

The framework of bones that supports the lower part of the abdomen is called the **pelvis**. The male pelvis is heart-shaped and narrow. The female pelvis is much wider and flatter, with a larger central cavity to accomodate a fetus during pregnancy and childbirth.

Label the parts of the pelvis.

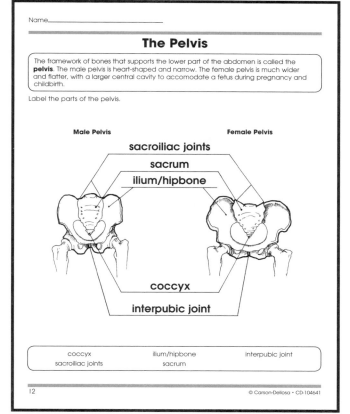

Male Pelvis   Female Pelvis

sacroiliac joints

sacrum

ilium/hipbone

coccyx

interpubic joint

coccyx	ilium/hipbone	interpubic joint
sacroiliac joints	sacrum	

Answer Key

Name_____

Bones of the Arm

Label the different arm bones and regions.

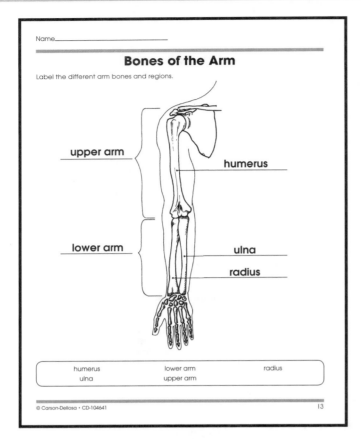

upper arm

humerus

lower arm

ulna

radius

humerus	lower arm	radius
ulna	upper arm	

13

Name_____

Bones Review

Cut out the skeleton and glue it together. Label the skeleton on the lines drawn on the bones using the words in the word bank.

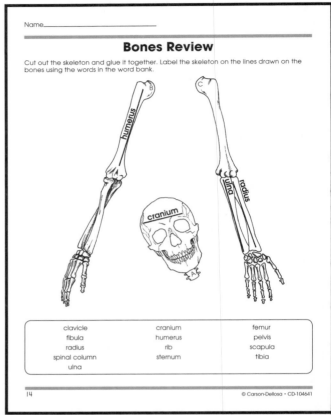

clavicle	cranium	femur
fibula	humerus	pelvis
radius	rib	scapula
spinal column	sternum	tibia
ulna		

14

Name_____

Bones Review (con't.)

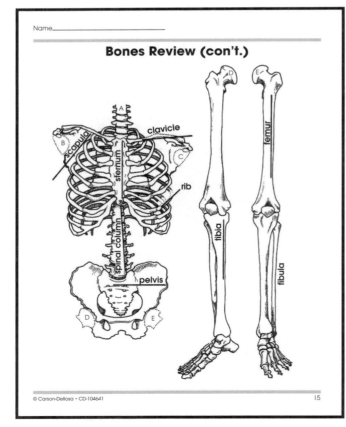

clavicle

scapula

sternum

rib

spinal column

pelvis

femur

tibia

fibula

15

Name_____

Skeletal System Crossword

Use the word bank to complete the puzzle.

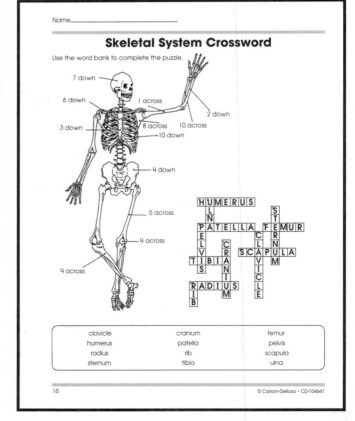

7 down

6 down

1 across

2 down

3 down

8 across

10 across

10 down

4 down

5 across

4 across

9 across

```
H U M E R U S       S
U                   T
L   P A T E L L A   F E M U R
N   E       C       R
A   L   C   L   S C A P U L A
    V   R   A       N
T I B I A   V       U
    S   A N I U M
    R A D I U S     E
    I   M
    B
```

clavicle	cranium	femur
humerus	patella	pelvis
radius	rib	scapula
sternum	tibia	ulna

16

Answer Key

Inside Teeth

Teeth are made up of a number of layers. Label the layers and outside parts of the tooth.

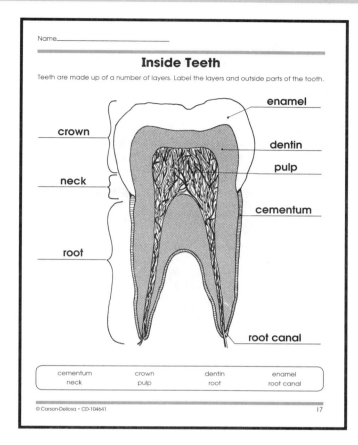

crown

enamel

dentin

pulp

neck

cementum

root

root canal

cementum	crown	dentin	enamel
neck	pulp	root	root canal

17

Bites

Each of the diagrams illustrates a different **bite**. The bite is the angle at which the upper and lower teeth meet.

Label the kind of bite found in each left-hand picture. Then, draw a line from the bite on the left to the corresponding profile on the right.

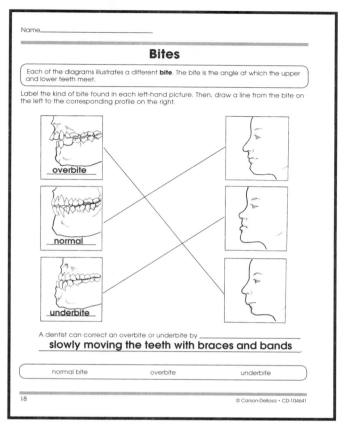

overbite

normal

underbite

A dentist can correct an overbite or underbite by _____
slowly moving the teeth with braces and bands

normal bite	overbite	underbite

18

Kinds of Teeth

There are four kinds of teeth in the human mouth. Label the adult teeth. Some words may be used more than once.

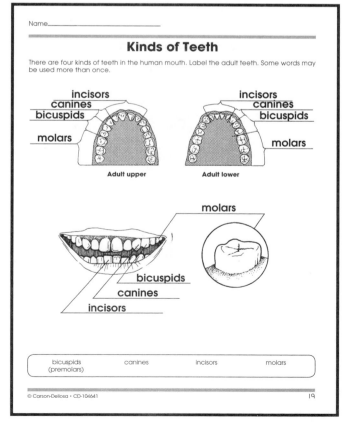

incisors
canines
bicuspids
molars

incisors
canines
bicuspids
molars

Adult upper   **Adult lower**

molars

bicuspids

canines

incisors

bicuspids (premolars)	canines	incisors	molars

19

Muscles

There are hundreds of muscle groups in the body. Label the muscles that appear on the surface of the body.

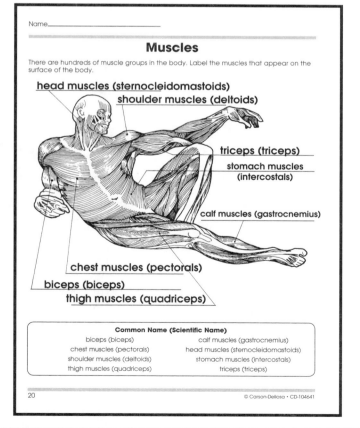

head muscles (sternocleidomastoids)

shoulder muscles (deltoids)

triceps (triceps)

stomach muscles (intercostals)

calf muscles (gastrocnemius)

chest muscles (pectorals)

biceps (biceps)

thigh muscles (quadriceps)

Common Name (Scientific Name)	
biceps (biceps)	calf muscles (gastrocnemius)
chest muscles (pectorals)	head muscles (sternocleidomastoids)
shoulder muscles (deltoids)	stomach muscles (intercostals)
thigh muscles (quadriceps)	triceps (triceps)

20

Answer Key

Name_____

Skeletal Muscles

Skeletal muscles are attached to the skeleton by **tendons**.

Label the parts of the arm.

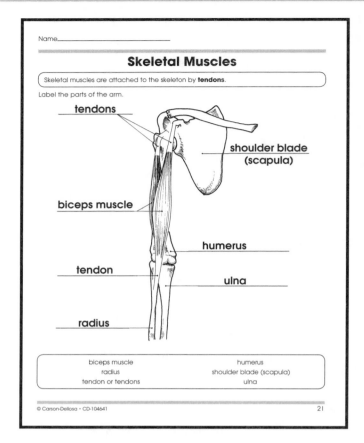

- tendons
- shoulder blade (scapula)
- biceps muscle
- humerus
- tendon
- ulna
- radius

biceps muscle	humerus
radius	shoulder blade (scapula)
tendon or tendons	ulna

Name_____

Muscle Types

Label the three different types of muscles and give an example of the kind of work they do. Then, label the muscle parts in the diagram. Some words may be used more than once.

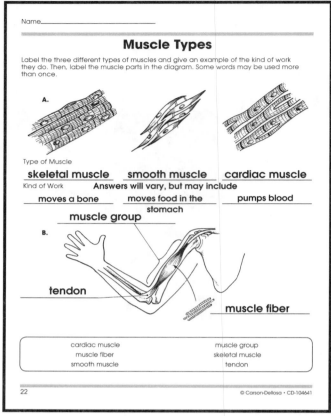

Type of Muscle

skeletal muscle	smooth muscle	cardiac muscle

Kind of Work   Answers will vary, but may include

moves a bone	moves food in the stomach	pumps blood

- muscle group
- tendon
- muscle fiber

cardiac muscle	muscle group
muscle fiber	skeletal muscle
smooth muscle	tendon

Name_____

Working Pairs

The muscles in both your upper arms and upper legs are very much alike. They both work in pairs to help raise and lower the limbs. Label the parts of each "working pair."

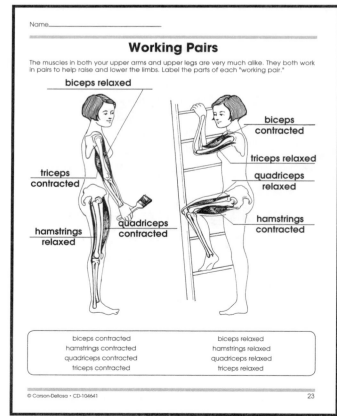

- biceps relaxed
- biceps contracted
- triceps relaxed
- quadriceps relaxed
- triceps contracted
- hamstrings contracted
- hamstrings relaxed
- quadriceps contracted

biceps contracted	biceps relaxed
hamstrings contracted	hamstrings relaxed
quadriceps contracted	quadriceps relaxed
triceps contracted	triceps relaxed

Name_____

The Circulatory System

Label the parts of the circulatory system.

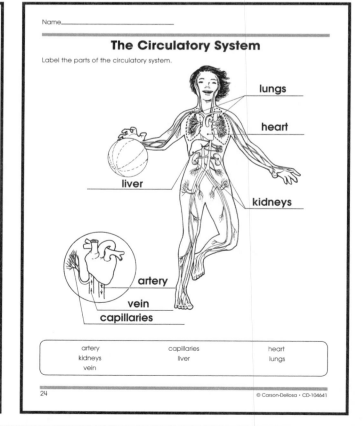

- lungs
- heart
- liver
- kidneys
- artery
- vein
- capillaries

artery	capillaries	heart
kidneys	liver	lungs
vein		

Answer Key

Name_____

Veins and Arteries

Arteries

Draw arrows on the arteries showing the flow of blood away from the heart.

Veins

Draw arrows on the veins showing the flow of blood back to the heart.

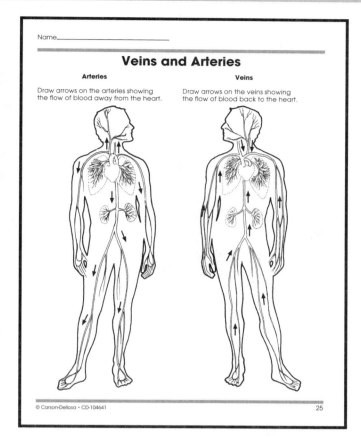

25

Name_____

The Heart

Label the parts of the heart.

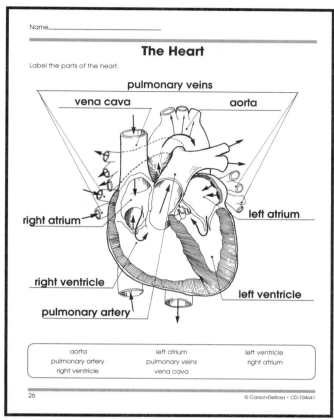

aorta	left atrium	left ventricle
pulmonary artery	pulmonary veins	right atrium
right ventricle	vena cava	

26

Name_____

The Heart

The heart has the job of pumping blood to the parts of the body. Label the parts of the heart and the location of the flow of blood.

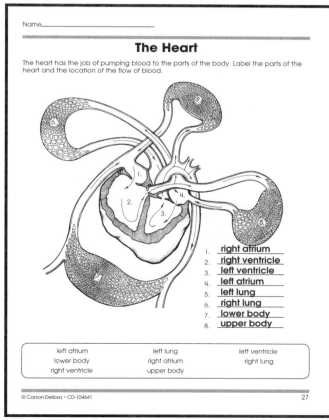

1. right atrium
2. right ventricle
3. left ventricle
4. left atrium
5. left lung
6. right lung
7. lower body
8. upper body

left atrium	left lung	left ventricle
lower body	right atrium	right lung
right ventricle	upper body	

27

Name_____

Pressure Points

When a person is cut severely and begins to bleed, it is time for quick action. First aid for severe bleeding involves applying pressure over the wound. Sometimes, it is possible to press the artery above the wound against the bone behind it to stop the bleeding. This place is called a **pressure point**. A pressure point is also an excellent location to take a person's pulse.

Place an **X** on the pressure points behind the knee, in the bend of the elbow, on the inside of the thigh, on the neck, on top of the foot, and on the wrist.

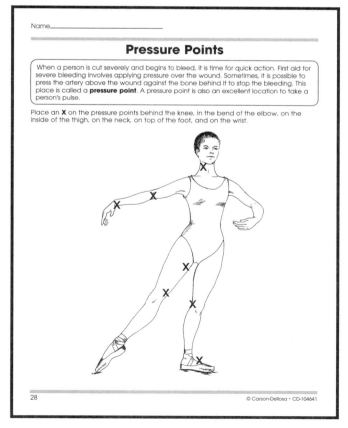

28

Answer Key

Circulatory System Crossword

Name_____

Use the word bank to complete the puzzle.

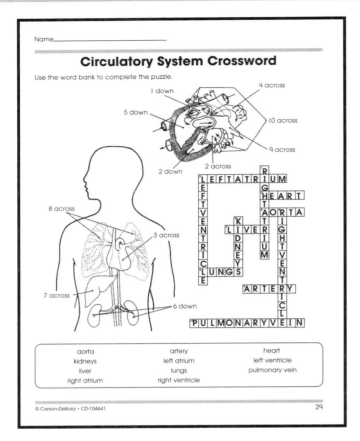

aorta	artery	heart
kidneys	left atrium	left ventricle
liver	lungs	pulmonary vein
right atrium	right ventricle	

The Respiratory System

Name_____

Label the parts of the respiratory system.

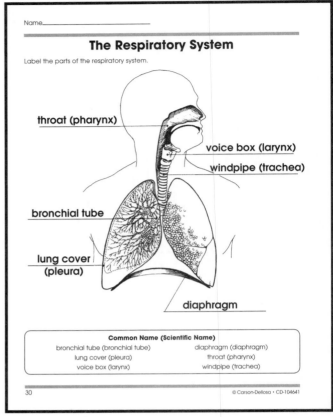

Common Name (Scientific Name)

bronchial tube (bronchial tube)	diaphragm (diaphragm)
lung cover (pleura)	throat (pharynx)
voice box (larynx)	windpipe (trachea)

The Lungs

Name_____

Label the parts of the lungs.

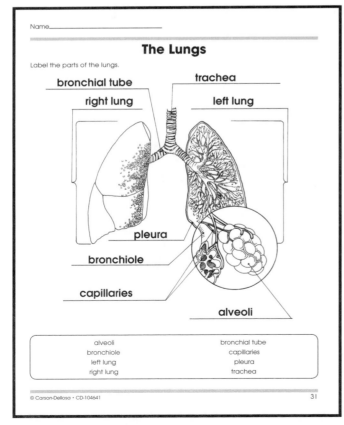

alveoli	bronchial tube
bronchiole	capillaries
left lung	pleura
right lung	trachea

Breathing

Name_____

Humans breathe in and breathe out almost 20,000 times each day. Label these pictures **inhale** (breathing in) or **exhale** (breathing out). Label the other parts of the breathing process.

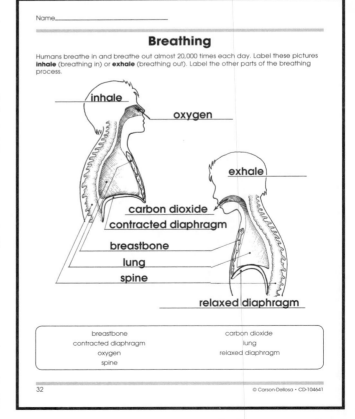

breastbone	carbon dioxide
contracted diaphragm	lung
oxygen	relaxed diaphragm
spine	

Answer Key

Respiratory System Crossword

Use the word bank to complete the puzzle.

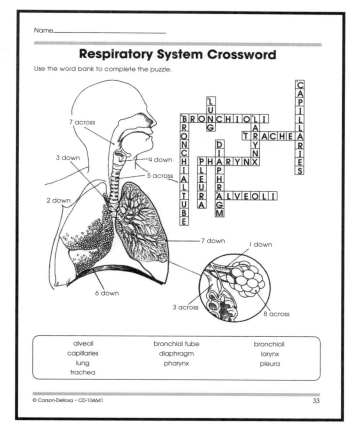

alveoli	bronchial tube	bronchioli
capillaries	diaphragm	larynx
lung	pharynx	pleura
trachea		

The Digestive System

Label the parts of the digestive system.

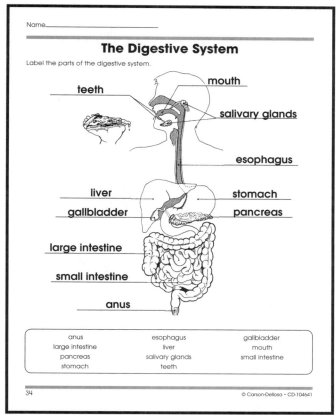

teeth — mouth — salivary glands — esophagus — liver — stomach — gallbladder — pancreas — large intestine — small intestine — anus

anus	esophagus	gallbladder
large intestine	liver	mouth
pancreas	salivary glands	small intestine
stomach	teeth	

The Alimentary Canal

The main part of the digestive system is the **alimentary canal**, a tube which starts at the mouth and travels through the body, ending at the anus.

Label the parts of the alimentary canal.

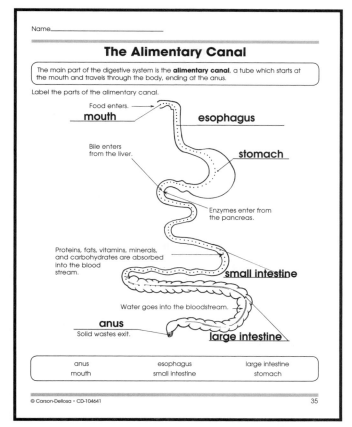

Food enters. — **mouth** — **esophagus** — Bile enters from the liver. — **stomach** — Enzymes enter from the pancreas. — Proteins, fats, vitamins, minerals, and carbohydrates are absorbed into the blood stream. — **small intestine** — Water goes into the bloodstream. — **anus** — Solid wastes exit. — **large intestine**

| anus | esophagus | large intestine |
| mouth | small intestine | stomach |

The Stomach

The **stomach** is the widest part of the alimentary canal. The stomach has three layers of muscles that allow it to contract in different directions. The contracting motion mashes food and mixes it with digestive juices.

Label the parts of the stomach and the tubes leading into and out of the stomach.

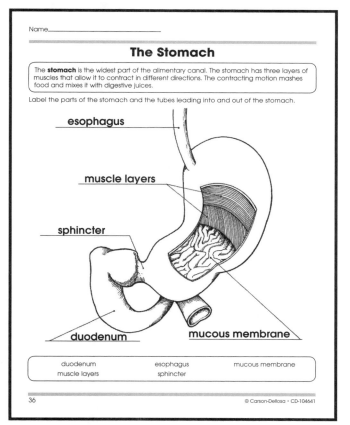

esophagus — **muscle layers** — **sphincter** — **duodenum** — **mucous membrane**

| duodenum | esophagus | mucous membrane |
| muscle layers | sphincter | |

Answer Key

Name_____

Digestion in the Mouth

Label the parts of the digestive system located in and around the mouth.

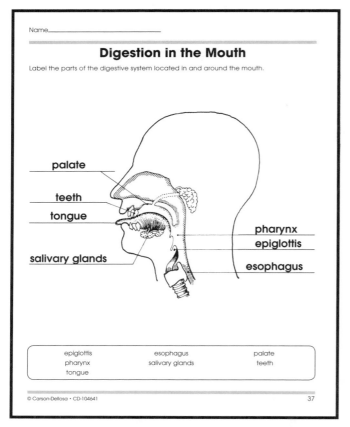

palate

teeth

tongue

salivary glands

pharynx

epiglottis

esophagus

epiglottis	esophagus	palate
pharynx	salivary glands	teeth
tongue		

© Carson-Dellosa • CD-104641   37

Name_____

The Pancreas, Liver, and Gallbladder

Label these organs that aid in digestion.

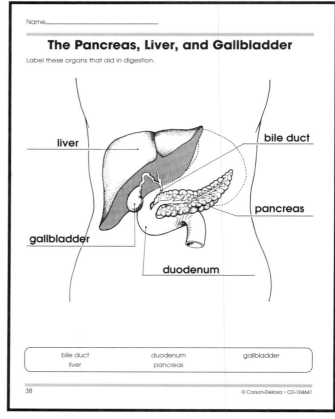

liver

bile duct

pancreas

gallbladder

duodenum

bile duct	duodenum	gallbladder
liver	pancreas	

38   © Carson-Dellosa • CD-104641

Name_____

Inside the Mouth

Label the parts of the mouth.

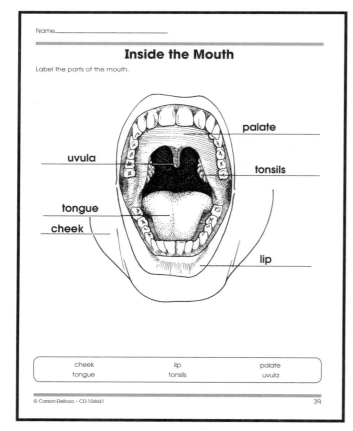

palate

uvula

tonsils

tongue

cheek

lip

cheek	lip	palate
tongue	tonsils	uvula

© Carson-Dellosa • CD-104641   39

Name_____

The Alimentary Canal

Label each part of the digestive system and draw a line to match the description to the part of the digestive system.

entrance to food tube; chews food

stores food for 3–4 hours while digestion occurs; churning breaks down proteins

opening for waste exit

20-foot-long tube for final digestion

muscular tube that squeezes food down to the stomach

stores solid waste; removes water

first part of small intestine; food enters it from the stomach

makes chemicals to break down food

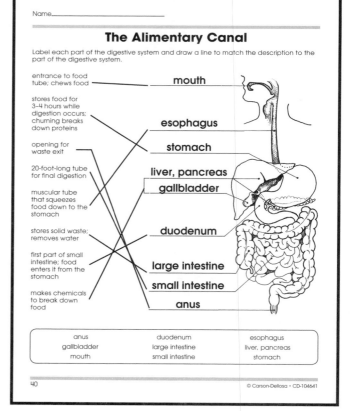

mouth

esophagus

stomach

liver, pancreas

gallbladder

duodenum

large intestine

small intestine

anus

anus	duodenum	esophagus
gallbladder	large intestine	liver, pancreas
mouth	small intestine	stomach

40   © Carson-Dellosa • CD-104641

Answer Key

Digestive System Crossword

Use the word bank to complete the puzzle.

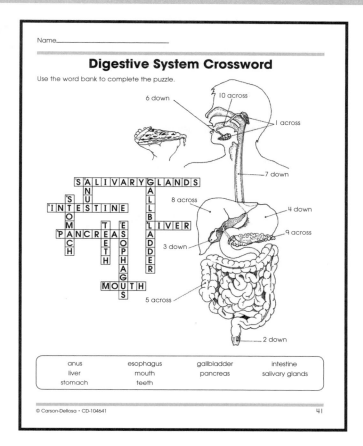

6 down
10 across
1 across
7 down

```
      S A L I V A R Y G L A N D S
      N               A
  S U I N T E S T I N E   L
  T   U           T   L
  P A N C R E A S T E   B
  M   C       E S     A L I V E R
  A   H       T O     D
  C           E P     D
  H             H     E
                A     R
                G
                U
                M O U T H
                S
```

8 across
4 down
9 across
3 down
5 across
2 down

anus	esophagus	gallbladder	intestine
liver	mouth	pancreas	salivary glands
stomach	teeth		

The Urinary System

Label the parts of the urinary system.

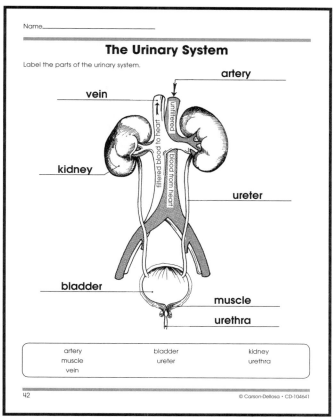

- artery
- vein
- unfiltered blood to heart
- filtered blood from heart
- kidney
- ureter
- bladder
- muscle
- urethra

artery	bladder	kidney
muscle	ureter	urethra
vein		

Waste Removal

The important job of removing bodily wastes is performed by the skin and the organs of the urinary and respiratory systems.

Label the excretory organs. Then, complete the chart by checking the boxes to show the function(s) of each organ.

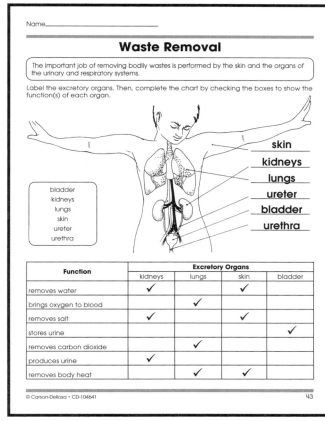

- skin
- kidneys
- lungs
- ureter
- bladder
- urethra

Word bank:
bladder
kidneys
lungs
skin
ureter
urethra

Function	Excretory Organs			
	kidneys	lungs	skin	bladder
removes water	✓		✓	
brings oxygen to blood		✓		
removes salt	✓		✓	
stores urine				✓
removes carbon dioxide		✓		
produces urine	✓			
removes body heat		✓	✓	

The Central Nervous System

Label the parts of the central nervous system.

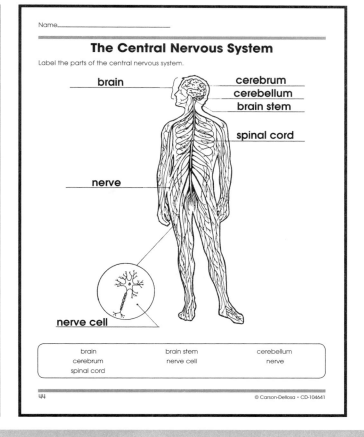

- brain
- cerebrum
- cerebellum
- brain stem
- spinal cord
- nerve
- nerve cell

brain	brain stem	cerebellum
cerebrum	nerve cell	nerve
spinal cord		

Answer Key

Neurons

Name_____

Label the parts of a neuron.

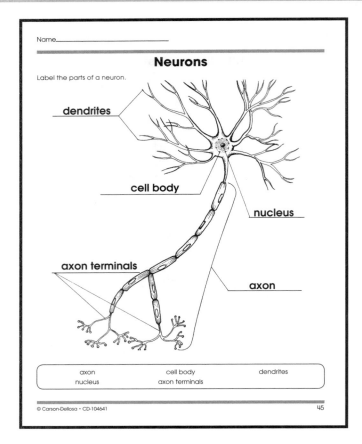

axon	cell body	dendrites
nucleus	axon terminals	

Transmitters of Impulses

Name_____

Neurons act as "go-betweens" in the sending and receiving of impulses within the nervous system. The diagrams illustrate how impulses pass from one neuron to another.

Label the parts of the diagram.

Synapse

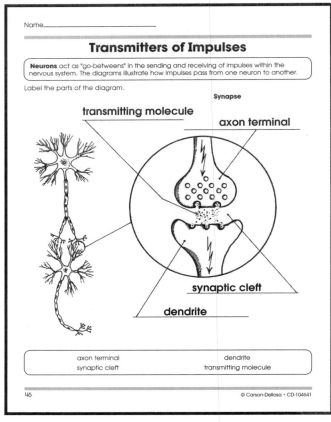

axon terminal	dendrite
synaptic cleft	transmitting molecule

The Brain

Name_____

Label the parts of the brain.

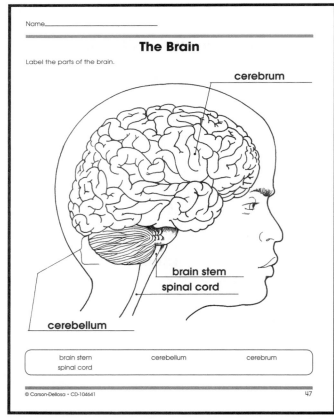

brain stem	cerebellum	cerebrum
spinal cord		

The Nervous System

Name_____

Two of the nervous systems in the human body are the **central** and the **peripheral**.

Label these two systems and their parts.

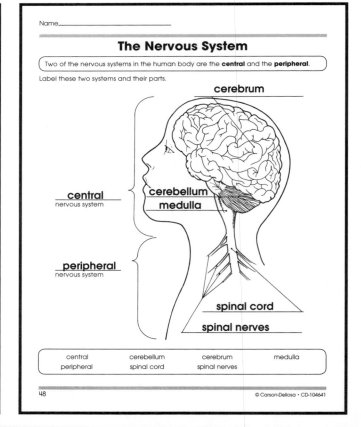

central	cerebellum	cerebrum	medulla
peripheral	spinal cord	spinal nerves	

Answer Key

The Nervous System at Work

Write the letter of each function next to its matching part. Then, draw a line from the pictured part of the nervous system to its function.

Part

1. cerebrum   **b**
2. cerebellum   **a**
3. medulla   **d**
4. spinal cord   **e**
5. spinal nerves   **c**

Functions

a. It controls balance and muscular coordination.

b. It controls thought, voluntary movement, memory and learning, and also processes information from the senses.

c. They carry impulses between the spinal cord and body parts.

d. It controls breathing, heartbeat, and other vital body processes.

e. It relays impulses between the brain and other parts of the body.

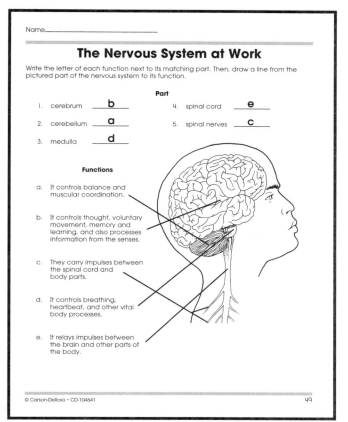

49

Nervous System Functions

Label the parts of the nervous system.

a. **cerebrum**
b. **cerebellum**
c. **medulla**
d. **spinal cord**
e. **spinal nerves**

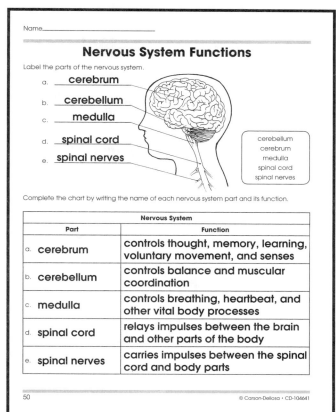

cerebellum
cerebrum
medulla
spinal cord
spinal nerves

Complete the chart by writing the name of each nervous system part and its function.

Nervous System	
Part	**Function**
a. **cerebrum**	controls thought, memory, learning, voluntary movement, and senses
b. **cerebellum**	controls balance and muscular coordination
c. **medulla**	controls breathing, heartbeat, and other vital body processes
d. **spinal cord**	relays impulses between the brain and other parts of the body
e. **spinal nerves**	carries impulses between the spinal cord and body parts

50

The Autonomic Nervous System

The **autonomic nervous system** works almost independently of the central nervous system. It controls the life-sustaining functions of the body such as breathing, digestion, and heartbeat. These organs and muscle tissues work involuntarily.

Label the parts of the autonomic nervous system.

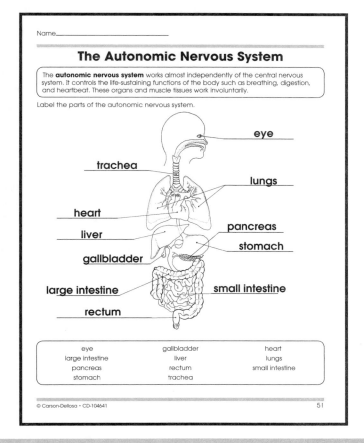

eye

trachea

lungs

heart

liver

pancreas

stomach

gallbladder

large intestine

small intestine

rectum

eye	gallbladder	heart
large intestine	liver	lungs
pancreas	rectum	small intestine
stomach	trachea	

51

Nervous System Crossword

Use the word bank to complete the puzzle.

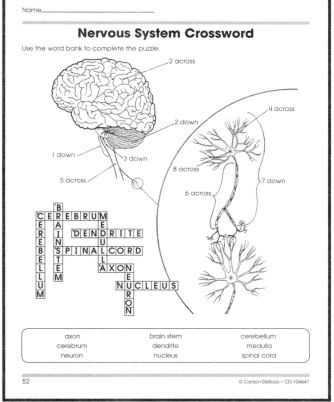

2 across
2 down
4 across
1 down
3 down
8 across
5 across
7 down
6 across

Crossword answers:
CEREBRUM
BRAINSTEM
CEREBELLUM
DENDRITE
SPINALCORD
AXON
NUCLEUS
NEURON

axon	brain stem	cerebellum
cerebrum	dendrite	medulla
neuron	nucleus	spinal cord

52

Answer Key

Name

The Endocrine System

The endocrine glands help control many of the body's functions. Label the glands of the endocrine system.

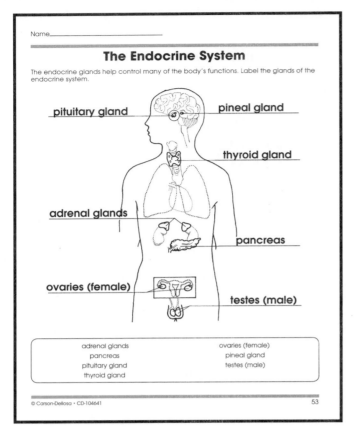

pituitary gland

pineal gland

thyroid gland

adrenal glands

pancreas

ovaries (female)

testes (male)

adrenal glands	ovaries (female)
pancreas	pineal gland
pituitary gland	testes (male)
thyroid gland	

Name

Glands

Draw a line from the name of the gland to its picture and from the picture of the gland to its function.

Gland

Function

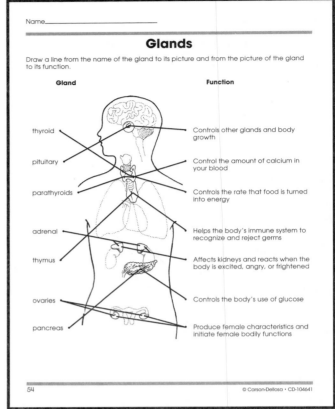

thyroid

pituitary

parathyroids

adrenal

thymus

ovaries

pancreas

Controls other glands and body growth

Control the amount of calcium in your blood

Controls the rate that food is turned into energy

Helps the body's immune system to recognize and reject germs

Affects kidneys and reacts when the body is excited, angry, or frightened

Controls the body's use of glucose

Produce female characteristics and initiate female bodily functions

---

Name

Endocrine Glands

Label the glands in the endocrine system.

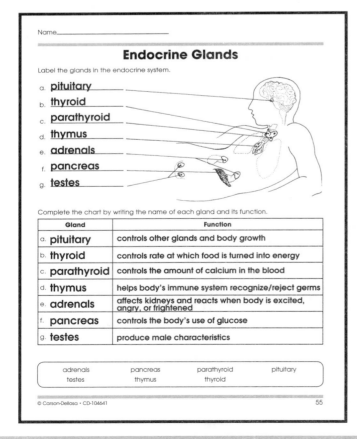

a. pituitary

b. thyroid

c. parathyroid

d. thymus

e. adrenals

f. pancreas

g. testes

Complete the chart by writing the name of each gland and its function.

Gland	Function
a. pituitary	controls other glands and body growth
b. thyroid	controls rate at which food is turned into energy
c. parathyroid	controls the amount of calcium in the blood
d. thymus	helps body's immune system recognize/reject germs
e. adrenals	affects kidneys and reacts when body is excited, angry, or frightened
f. pancreas	controls the body's use of glucose
g. testes	produce male characteristics

adrenals	pancreas	parathyroid	pituitary
testes	thymus	thyroid	

Name

The Sensory Systems

The brain gets information from outside the body through many different sense organs. Label the different sense organs and the nerve cell pictured on this page.

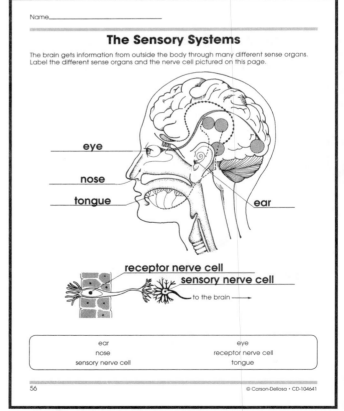

eye

nose

tongue

ear

receptor nerve cell

sensory nerve cell

to the brain

ear	eye
nose	receptor nerve cell
sensory nerve cell	tongue

Answer Key

Name_____

Taste

The tongue can sense four basic tastes—sweet, sour, bitter, and salty. Label the different sense areas of the tongue and the different parts of this sense organ.

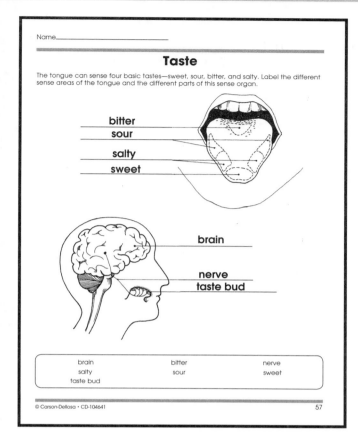

bitter
sour
salty
sweet

brain

nerve
taste bud

brain	bitter	nerve
salty	sour	sweet
taste bud		

57

Name_____

The Nose

Label the parts of the nose.

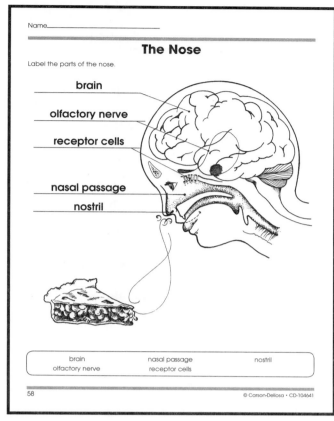

brain

olfactory nerve

receptor cells

nasal passage

nostril

brain	nasal passage	nostril
olfactory nerve	receptor cells	

58

Name_____

The Ear

Label the parts of the ear.

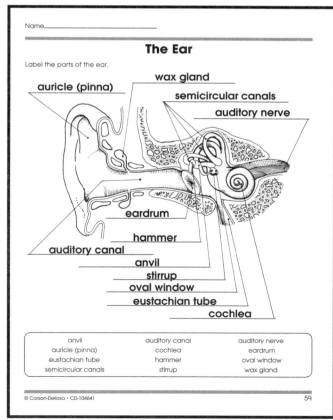

auricle (pinna)

wax gland
semicircular canals
auditory nerve

eardrum
hammer
auditory canal
anvil
stirrup
oval window
eustachian tube
cochlea

anvil	auditory canal	auditory nerve
auricle (pinna)	cochlea	eardrum
eustachian tube	hammer	oval window
semicircular canals	stirrup	wax gland

59

Name_____

The Outer Ear

Label the three major regions of the ear. Then, label the parts of the outer ear.

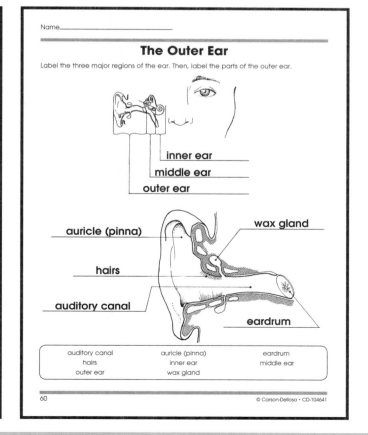

inner ear
middle ear
outer ear

auricle (pinna)

wax gland

hairs

auditory canal

eardrum

auditory canal	auricle (pinna)	eardrum
hairs	inner ear	middle ear
outer ear	wax gland	

60

Answer Key

The Middle Ear

Label the three major regions of the ear. Then, label the parts of the middle ear.

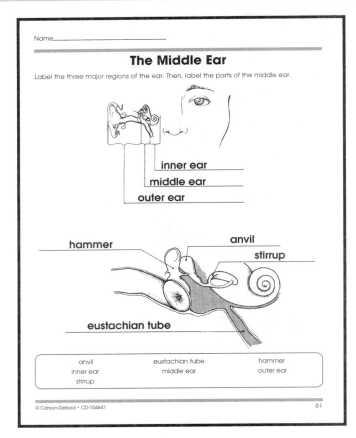

inner ear
middle ear
outer ear

hammer
anvil
stirrup

eustachian tube

anvil	eustachian tube	hammer
inner ear	middle ear	outer ear
stirrup		

The Inner Ear

Label the three major regions of the ear. Then, label the parts of the inner ear.

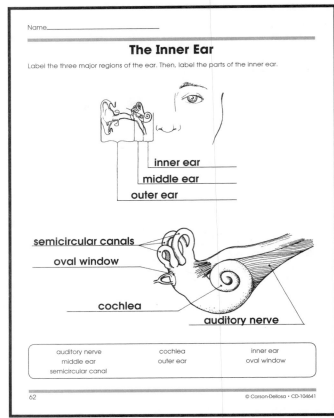

inner ear
middle ear
outer ear

semicircular canals
oval window

cochlea
auditory nerve

auditory nerve	cochlea	inner ear
middle ear	outer ear	oval window
semicircular canal		

Ear, Nose, and Throat

The ears, nose, mouth, and throat are all connected to each other. Label the parts in the diagram.

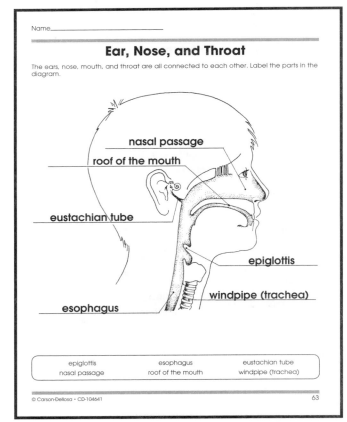

nasal passage
roof of the mouth

eustachian tube

esophagus

epiglottis

windpipe (trachea)

| epiglottis | esophagus | eustachian tube |
| nasal passage | roof of the mouth | windpipe (trachea) |

The Eye

Label the parts of the eye. Some words may be used more than once.

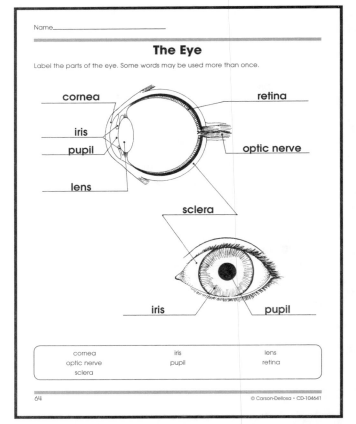

cornea
retina

iris
pupil
optic nerve

lens

sclera

iris
pupil

cornea	iris	lens
optic nerve	pupil	retina
sclera		

Answer Key

Name_____

Inside the Eye

Label the parts of the eye.

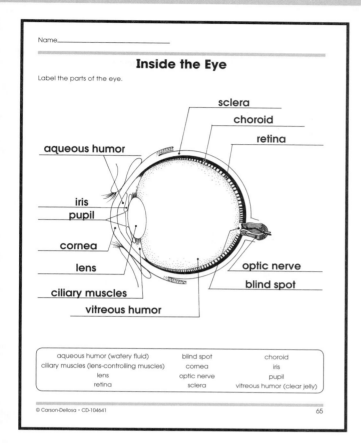

- sclera
- choroid
- retina
- aqueous humor
- iris
- pupil
- cornea
- lens
- ciliary muscles
- vitreous humor
- optic nerve
- blind spot

aqueous humor (watery fluid)	blind spot	choroid
ciliary muscles (lens-controlling muscles)	cornea	iris
lens	optic nerve	pupil
retina	sclera	vitreous humor (clear jelly)

Name_____

Eye-to-Brain Connection

Your eyes gather the rays of light coming off of an object. They change the light rays into nerve impulses, but your brain interprets these impulses and "draws" a picture of the image.

Label the parts of this "eye-to-brain connection."

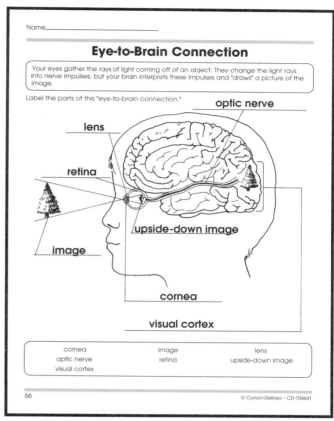

- optic nerve
- lens
- retina
- upside-down image
- image
- cornea
- visual cortex

cornea	image	lens
optic nerve	retina	upside-down image
visual cortex		

Name_____

Eye Protection

The eyeball is very well protected. Label the parts of the eye and those that help protect it.

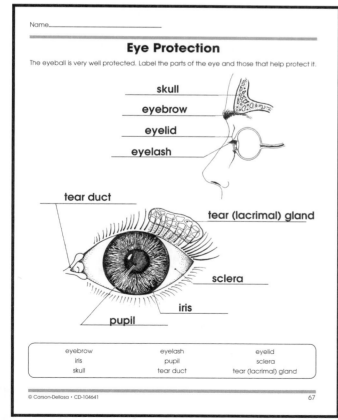

- skull
- eyebrow
- eyelid
- eyelash
- tear duct
- tear (lacrimal) gland
- sclera
- iris
- pupil

eyebrow	eyelash	eyelid
iris	pupil	sclera
skull	tear duct	tear (lacrimal) gland

Name_____

The Eye and the Camera

A camera is very similar to the eye. Label the parts of the eye and the camera. Then, write the job of each part. Some words may be used more than once.

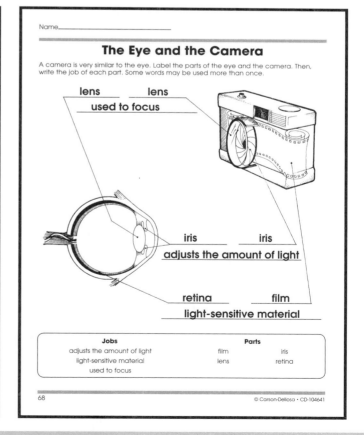

- lens / lens
- used to focus
- iris / iris
- adjusts the amount of light
- retina / film
- light-sensitive material

Jobs		Parts	
adjusts the amount of light		film	iris
light-sensitive material		lens	retina
used to focus			

Answer Key

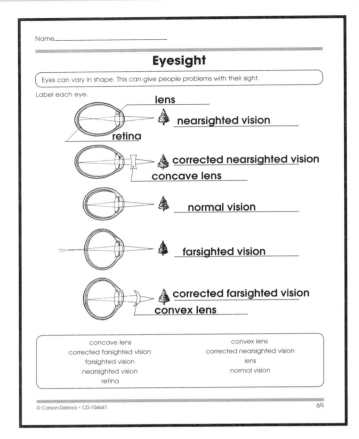
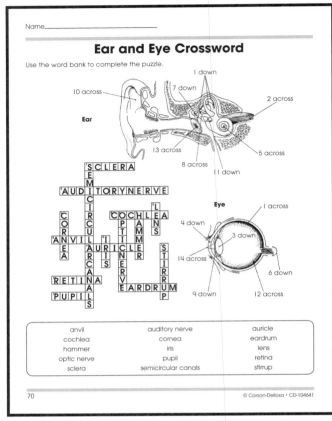
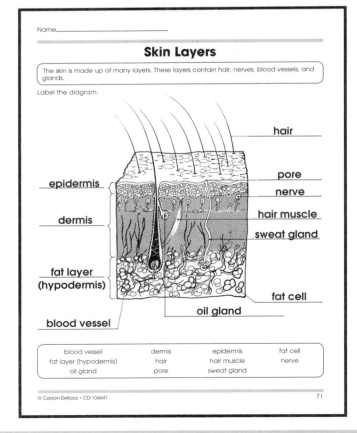
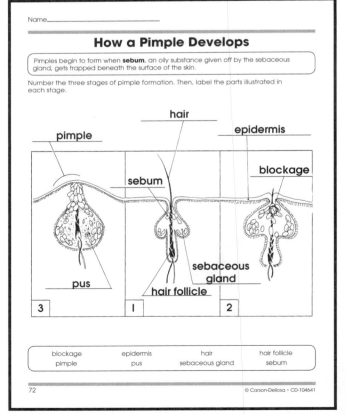

Answer Key

Temperature Regulation

On cold days, the skin has a way to keep in the body's warmth. On hot days, the skin can cool the body.

Label the pictures **warm day** or **cool day.** Then, label the parts of the skin.

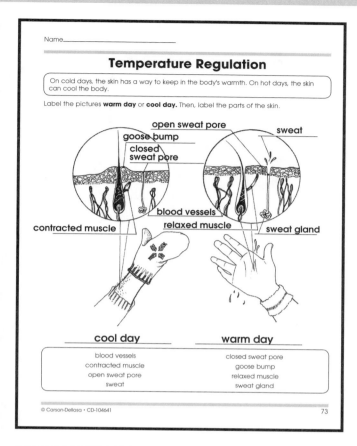

- open sweat pore
- goose bump
- closed sweat pore
- sweat
- blood vessels
- contracted muscle
- relaxed muscle
- sweat gland

cool day

warm day

blood vessels	closed sweat pore
contracted muscle	goose bump
open sweat pore	relaxed muscle
sweat	sweat gland

© Carson-Dellosa • CD-104641

73

Body Tissues

Many of the body's organs are made of a variety of tissues working together. There are four kinds of tissue: **connective, epithelial, muscle,** and **nerve.** Each has a specialized function.

Study the pictures and read the descriptions. Write the name of each tissue beneath its description and label the tissue parts in each picture.

Composed of relatively few cells and surrounded by larger amounts of nonliving material; supports and connects other tissues

connective tissue

Made up of cells that can contract and relax; allows the body to make internal and external movements

muscle tissue

Specialized cells which carry electrical signals between the brain and other parts of the body

nerve tissue

Tightly packed cells forming a covering for the skin and lining the hollow internal organs

epithelial tissue

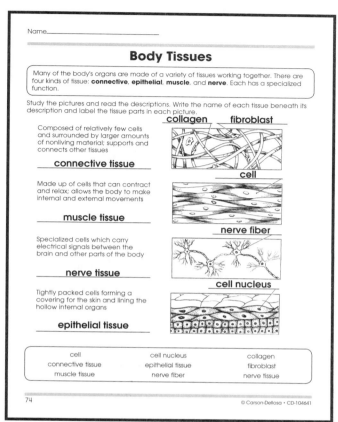

- collagen
- fibroblast
- cell
- nerve fiber
- cell nucleus

cell	cell nucleus	collagen
connective tissue	epithelial tissue	fibroblast
muscle tissue	nerve fiber	nerve tissue

74

© Carson-Dellosa • CD-104641

Fingerprints

The ridges in fingertips form unique patterns. No two people have the same pattern, not even identical twins. The ridges on fingers form three main groups of patterns—the **arch,** the **loop,** and the **whorl.**

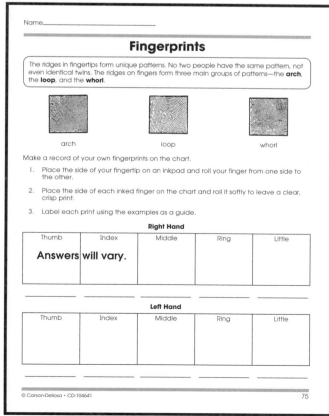

arch

loop

whorl

Make a record of your own fingerprints on the chart.

1. Place the side of your fingertip on an inkpad and roll your finger from one side to the other.

2. Place the side of each inked finger on the chart and roll it softly to leave a clear, crisp print.

3. Label each print using the examples as a guide.

Right Hand

Thumb	Index	Middle	Ring	Little
Answers will vary.				

Left Hand

Thumb	Index	Middle	Ring	Little

© Carson-Dellosa • CD-104641

75

Toenails and Fingernails

Nails are a specialized part of your skin that protect the ends of your toes and fingers.

Label the parts of the nails. Words may be used more than once.

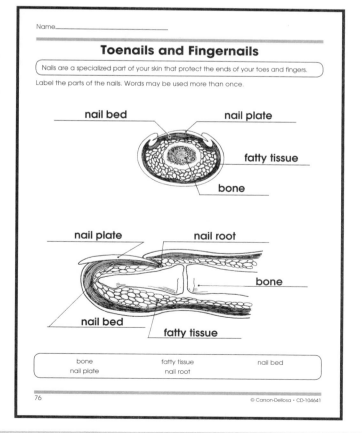

- nail bed
- nail plate
- fatty tissue
- bone
- nail plate
- nail root
- bone
- nail bed
- fatty tissue

bone	fatty tissue	nail bed
nail plate	nail root	

76

© Carson-Dellosa • CD-104641

© Carson-Dellosa • CD-104641

Answer Key

Reproductive System—Male

The purpose of the reproductive system is to create new life. Label the parts of the male reproductive system.

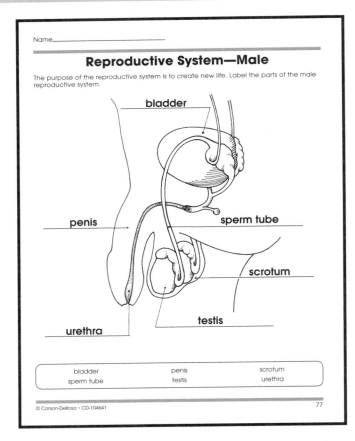

- bladder
- penis
- sperm tube
- scrotum
- testis
- urethra

| bladder | penis | scrotum |
| sperm tube | testis | urethra |

Reproductive System—Female

The purpose of the reproductive system is to create new life. Label the parts of the female reproductive system.

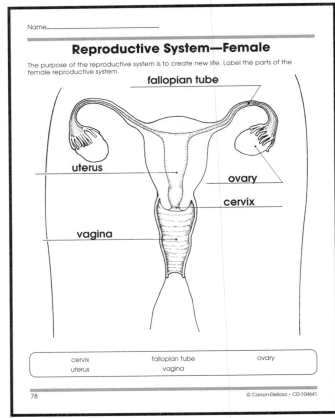

- fallopian tube
- uterus
- ovary
- cervix
- vagina

| cervix | fallopian tube | ovary |
| uterus | vagina | |

New Life

From the time of conception, a single cell divides and keeps dividing until it forms the six trillion cells of a human newborn baby. This development takes nine months.

Write the matching description of a baby's development under each picture.

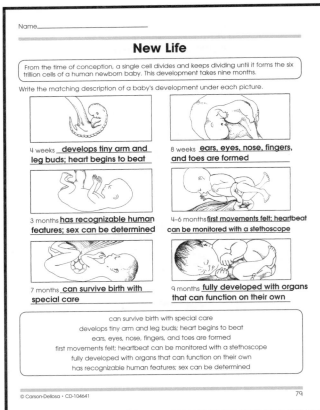

4 weeks **develops tiny arm and leg buds; heart begins to beat**

8 weeks **ears, eyes, nose, fingers, and toes are formed**

3 months **has recognizable human features; sex can be determined**

4–6 months **first movements felt; heartbeat can be monitored with a stethoscope**

7 months **can survive birth with special care**

9 months **fully developed with organs that can function on their own**

> can survive birth with special care
> develops tiny arm and leg buds; heart begins to beat
> ears, eyes, nose, fingers, and toes are formed
> first movements felt; heartbeat can be monitored with a stethoscope
> fully developed with organs that can function on their own
> has recognizable human features; sex can be determined

Birth of a Baby

When a baby is fully developed within the uterus, a hormone in the pituitary gland stimulates the muscles of the uterus. These muscle contractions signal the beginning of labor. The opening to the uterus, the cervix, gradually enlarges to allow the baby to pass through. The amniotic sac that surrounds the baby will break, releasing a gush of amniotic fluid. After the baby is born, the placenta separates from the wall of the uterus and is pushed out by more muscle contractions.

Label the diagram of the birth of a baby.

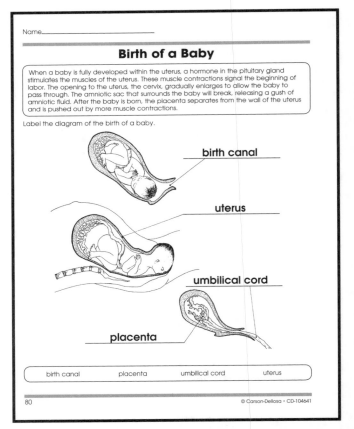

- birth canal
- uterus
- umbilical cord
- placenta

| birth canal | placenta | umbilical cord | uterus |

Answer Key

Genes

There are more than 40,000 **genes** that determine which traits each person has. These traits, such as dark hair or blue eyes, are inherited from parents. There are two strengths of traits: **dominant** is the strongest and **recessive** is the weakest.

Place checks in each chart to show which parent(s) would have the dominant or recessive genes in each category if the child had the dominant or recessive trait. Circle the traits you have inherited.

D = Dominant Trait   R = Recessive Trait

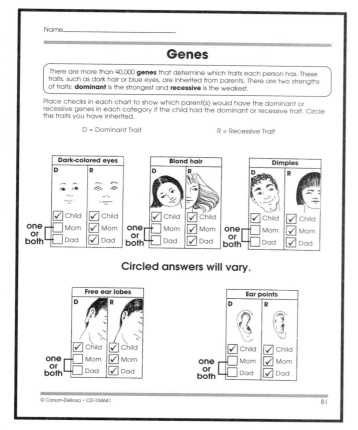

Circled answers will vary.

Genes (con't.)

D = Dominant Trait   R = Recessive Trait

Circled answers will vary.

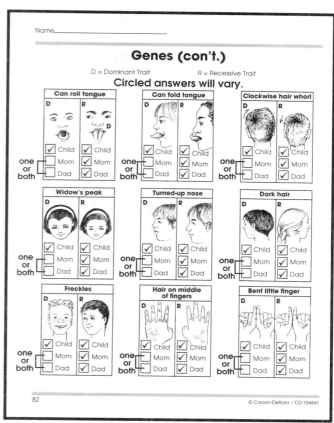

Inside the Head (Page A)

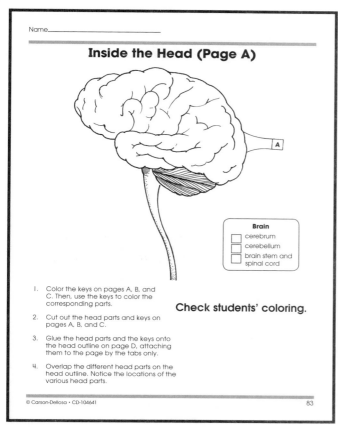

Brain
- [ ] cerebrum
- [ ] cerebellum
- [ ] brain stem and spinal cord

Check students' coloring.

1. Color the keys on pages A, B, and C. Then, use the keys to color the corresponding parts.
2. Cut out the head parts and keys on pages A, B, and C.
3. Glue the head parts and keys onto the head outline on page D, attaching them to the page by the tabs only.
4. Overlap the different head parts on the head outline. Notice the locations of the various head parts.

Inside the Head (Page B)

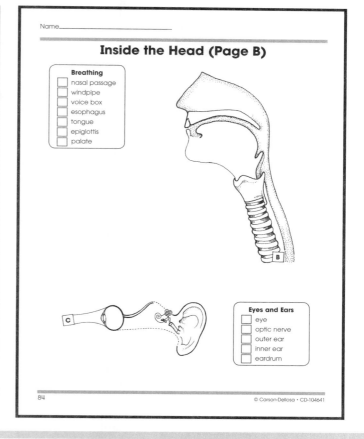

Breathing
- [ ] nasal passage
- [ ] windpipe
- [ ] voice box
- [ ] esophagus
- [ ] tongue
- [ ] epiglottis
- [ ] palate

Eyes and Ears
- [ ] eye
- [ ] optic nerve
- [ ] outer ear
- [ ] inner ear
- [ ] eardrum

Answer Key

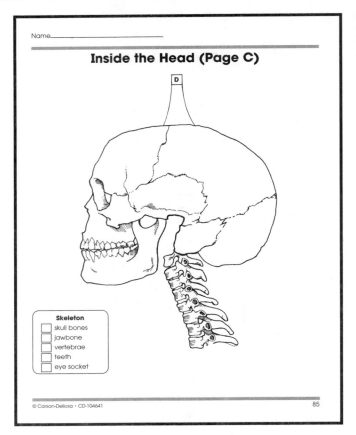
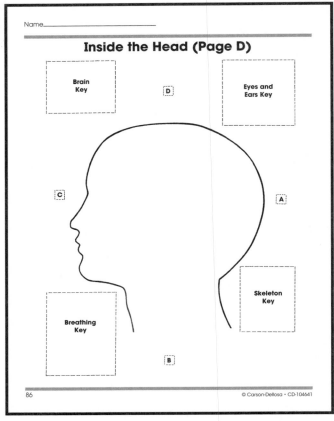
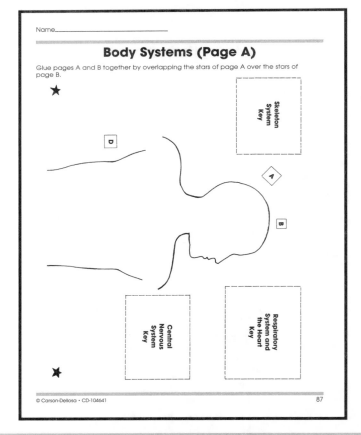
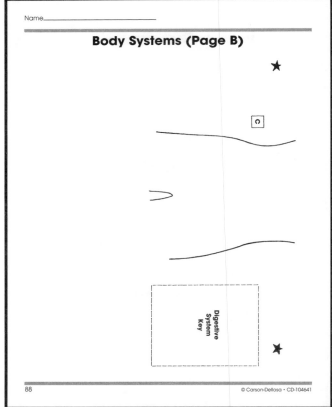

Answer Key

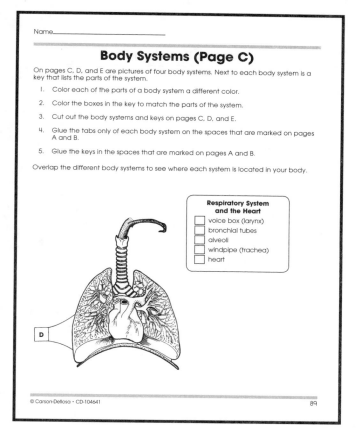

Name_____

Body Systems (Page C)

On pages C, D, and E are pictures of four body systems. Next to each body system is a key that lists the parts of the system.

1. Color each of the parts of a body system a different color.
2. Color the boxes in the key to match the parts of the system.
3. Cut out the body systems and keys on pages C, D, and E.
4. Glue the tabs only of each body system on the spaces that are marked on pages A and B.
5. Glue the keys in the spaces that are marked on pages A and B.

Overlap the different body systems to see where each system is located in your body.

Respiratory System and the Heart
- [ ] voice box (larynx)
- [ ] bronchial tubes
- [ ] alveoli
- [ ] windpipe (trachea)
- [ ] heart

© Carson-Dellosa • CD-104641   89

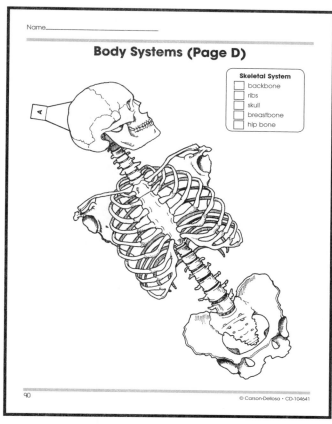

Name_____

Body Systems (Page D)

Skeletal System
- [ ] backbone
- [ ] ribs
- [ ] skull
- [ ] breastbone
- [ ] hip bone

90   © Carson-Dellosa • CD-104641

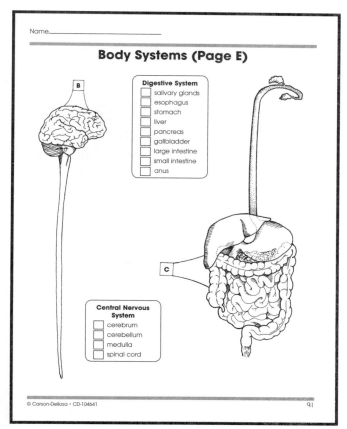

Name_____

Body Systems (Page E)

Digestive System
- [ ] salivary glands
- [ ] esophagus
- [ ] stomach
- [ ] liver
- [ ] pancreas
- [ ] gallbladder
- [ ] large intestine
- [ ] small intestine
- [ ] anus

Central Nervous System
- [ ] cerebrum
- [ ] cerebellum
- [ ] medulla
- [ ] spinal cord

© Carson-Dellosa • CD-104641   91

Name_____

Organ Systems

Place an **X** in the boxes that show to which system or systems each organ belongs.

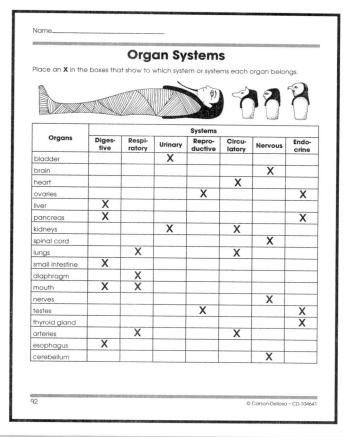

Organs	Systems						
	Diges-tive	Respi-ratory	Urinary	Repro-ductive	Circu-latory	Nervous	Endo-crine
bladder			X				
brain						X	
heart					X		
ovaries				X			X
liver	X						
pancreas	X						X
kidneys			X		X		
spinal cord						X	
lungs		X			X		
small intestine	X						
diaphragm		X					
mouth	X	X					
nerves						X	
testes				X			X
thyroid gland							X
arteries		X			X		
esophagus	X						
cerebellum						X	

92   © Carson-Dellosa • CD-104641

Answer Key

Human Body Crossword

Use the word bank to complete the puzzle.

Across

1. Outer layer of skin
4. The blood pump
6. Stores urine
10. The "bite" is the _____ of the teeth.
11. Opening to the uterus
12. Structure and bone system
13. The inside of the hand
14. Controls body growth and other glands
17. A break in a bone
20. Created by the rhythm of the heart
21. Female sex glands
22. Determine human traits

Down

1. Waste removal system
2. Outer layer of the tooth
3. Upper arm bone
5. Gland activated by excitement, anger, or fright
7. _____ fluid surrounds a fetus.
8. Long food tube
9. Joint found in elbow
12. Oily substance given off by the sebaceous gland
13. Gland which controls the body's use of glucose
15. Place where arteries are close to skin; place to take pulse
16. Muscles are attached to the skeleton by _____.
18. Male sex glands
19. Framework of bones that supports the lower part of the abdomen

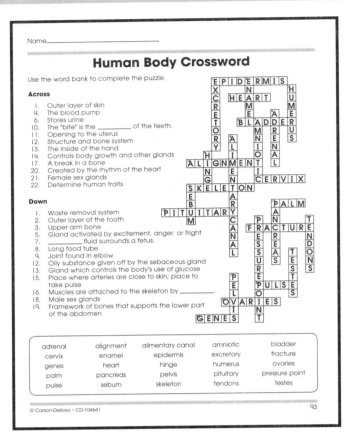

adrenal	alignment	alimentary canal	amniotic	bladder
cervix	enamel	epidermis	excretory	fracture
genes	heart	hinge	humerus	ovaries
palm	pancreas	pelvis	pituitary	pressure point
pulse	sebum	skeleton	tendons	testes

93

Experiment: Reaction Time

The time it takes for your sensory organs to send a message to your brain and your body to respond is called **reaction time**.

This experiment tests reaction time. Follow the directions.

Materials: 30cm metric ruler

Procedure:

1. Place your left arm on a table with your hand over the edge.
2. Space your thumb and index fingers about 4 cm apart.
3. Have a partner hold the ruler by the 30cm end, with the other end just above your open thumb and index finger.
4. Your partner will say "go" and drop the ruler.
5. Catch the ruler with your thumb and index finger as quickly as possible.
6. Check the distance fallen by taking a reading at the bottom of the index finger.
7. Record your results.
8. Repeat the procedure 10 times with each hand.

   Are you right-handed or left-handed? Which of your hands was the quickest?

   Did others find the same results?

   _____

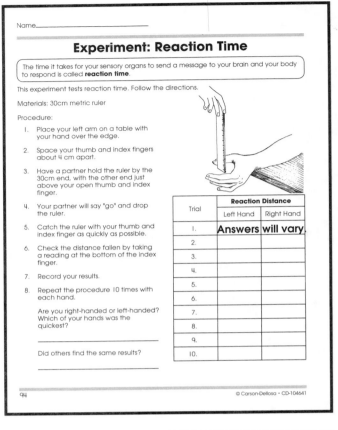

Trial	Reaction Distance	
	Left Hand	Right Hand
1.	**Answers**	**will vary.**
2.		
3.		
4.		
5.		
6.		
7.		
8.		
9.		
10.		

94

Experiment: Heart Rate

When the heart pumps, it forces blood out into the arteries. The walls of the arteries expand and contract to the rhythm of the heart, which creates a **pulse**.

You can feel your pulse where the arteries are close to the surface of the skin. Two good places to feel a pulse are on the inside of the wrist and on the neck to the side of the windpipe.

The type of activity you are doing can greatly affect the rate of your pulse. Try the experiments below. Complete the chart by counting the number of heart beats in 15 seconds and multiplying that number by 4 to get the pulse rate for 1 minute.

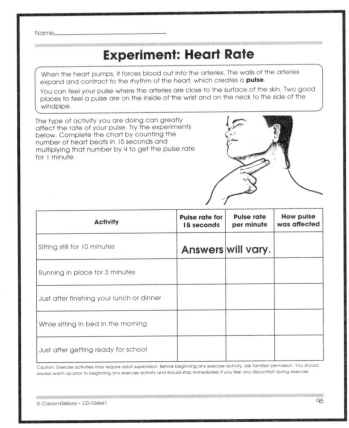

Activity	Pulse rate for 15 seconds	Pulse rate per minute	How pulse was affected
Sitting still for 10 minutes	**Answers**	**will vary.**	
Running in place for 3 minutes			
Just after finishing your lunch or dinner			
While sitting in bed in the morning			
Just after getting ready for school			

Caution: Exercise activities may require adult supervision. Before beginning any exercise activity, ask families' permission. You should always warm up prior to beginning any exercise activity and should stop immediately if you feel any discomfort during exercise.

95

Proper Portions

This graphic represents the portions recommended by the US Department of Agriculture.

Find Out

What foods do you eat each day? Choose a day and make a chart of what you eat. Record the kind of food and the number of servings.

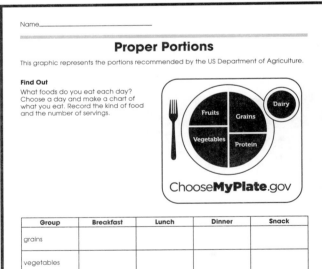

Group	Breakfast	Lunch	Dinner	Snack
grains				
vegetables				
fruits		**Answers**	**will vary.**	
protein				
dairy				
fats, oils, sweets				

How did you do? Compare your servings to the recommended proportions.

96

Answer Key

Name_____

Snacks and Nutrition

Some snack foods are better for you than others. Foods that contain smaller amounts of fat are usually much better for you.

Labels might not use the name **sugar** when they list sweeteners. Watch for other names for sugar, such as dextrose, lactose, corn syrup, fructose, molasses, and sucrose.

Snacker's Survey

Write the food group to which each snack belongs. Then, using a scale of 1–10, with 1 being the lowest, give each snack a taste score and a nutrition score.

Snack	Food Group	Taste Score	Nutrition Score
apple	fruits		
cheese	dairy		
cookie	sweets		
potato chips	grains, oils	Answers will vary.	
orange	fruits		
carrot	vegetables		
cake	sweets		
candy bar	sweets		
bagel	grains		
beef jerky	fats, meats		
popcorn	grains		
pretzels	grains		

Name_____

Nutrients

The body is made up of millions of cells that need food to stay alive. The body needs **nutrients** from foods to help the cells grow and repair themselves. Nutrients are divided into six major groups: **fats**, **proteins**, **carbohydrates**, **minerals**, **vitamins**, and **water**.

Read each clue. Identify the nutrient.

1. "I'm the body's building material. I make new tissue. There is plenty of me in milk, beans, meat, and peanuts."
   Who am I? __protein__

2. "I have energy for work and play. Find me in starchy foods such as pasta and potatoes."
   Who am I? __carbohydrate__

3. "I help build strong bones and teeth. I am important for healthy red blood. Find me in all four food groups."
   Who am I? __mineral__

4. "I am a concentrated source of energy. Find me in oily and greasy foods, such as bacon, salad dressing, and butter. I also help maintain healthy skin and hair."
   Who am I? __fat__

5. "I am one of the essential nutrients. I don't give any energy, but I do help the body get energy from the other nutrients."
   Who am I? __vitamin__

6. "I make up over half of human body weight. My job is to carry all of the good nutrients throughout the body. I also help the body to remove wastes."
   Who am I? __water__

Word Bank
carbohydrate
fat
mineral
protein
vitamin
water

Name_____

Nutrition Facts

Looking closely at the information on a cereal box provides interesting facts about the product.

Carefully read the nutrition facts shown for the cereal Corn Balls. Answer the questions. Compare these answers with the information found on a box of cereal you might eat for breakfast.

	Corn Balls	Your Cereal
What kind of grain is used?	corn	Answers will vary.
Is sugar used?	yes	
What position is sugar on the list of ingredients?	second	
List other sweeteners.	corn syrup, molasses	
How many calories are present per serving without milk?	210	
How many calories are present per serving when eaten with 1/2 cup of skim milk?	250	
How much protein is present per serving?	5 g	
How many vitamins and minerals does the cereal contain?	13	
How much cholesterol is in one serving?	0 mg	
How much fat is in one serving?	1 g	
How much carbohydrate is in one serving?	45 g	

Nutrition Facts
Serving Size 1 cup (55g)
Servings Per Package: About 12

	Cereal	Cereal With 1/2 Cup Skim Milk
Amount Per Serving		
Calories from Fat	210	250
Calories	10	10

%Daily Value**

Total Fat 1g*	2%	2%
Saturated Fat 0g	0%	0%
Trans Fat 0g		
Polyunsaturated Fat 0.5g		
Monounsaturated Fat 0g		
Cholesterol 0mg	0%	1%
Sodium 10mg	0%	3%
Potassium 180mg	5%	11%
Total Carbohydrate 45g	15%	17%
Dietary Fiber 6g	24%	24%
Soluble Fiber 1g		
Insoluble Fiber 5g		
Sugars 11g		
Other Carbohydrate 28g		
Protein 5g		

Calcium	2%	15%
Iron	10%	15%
Vitamin D	0%	10%
Thiamin	10%	10%
Riboflavin	4%	15%
Niacin	15%	15%
Vitamin B6	8%	10%
Folate (Folic Acid)	4%	6%
Vitamin B12	2%	10%
Phosphorus	15%	25%
Magnesium	10%	15%
Zinc	10%	15%
Copper	10%	10%

Not a significant source of Vitamin A and Vitamin C.

* Amount in cereal. One-half cup skim milk contributes an additional 40mg sodium, 6g total carbohydrate (6g sugars) and 4g protein.

** Percent Daily Values are based on a 2,000 calorie diet. Your daily values may be higher or lower depending on your calorie needs.

	Calories	2,000	2,500
Total Fat	Less than	65g	80g
Saturated Fat	Less than	20g	25g
Cholesterol	Less than	300mg	300mg
Sodium	Less than	2,400mg	2,400mg
Potassium		3,500mg	3,500mg
Total Carbohydrate		300g	375g
Dietary Fiber		25g	30g

Calories per gram: Fat 9 • Carbohydrate 4 • Protein 4

Ingredients: Corn, sugar, corn syrup, molasses, salt, annatto color.

Name_____

Burning Calories

Regular exercise strengthens the heart and helps burn calories to maintain a healthy weight.

The activities named below list the number of calories burned by a 150-pound person when he or she engages in an activity for 30 minutes. Circle the seven activities below that burn the most calories.

Activity	Calories Burned in 30 Minutes	Activity	Calories Burned in 30 Minutes
cross country skiing	210	homework	55
running (7 mph)	275	raquetball	365
shuffleboard	90	baseball	60
bicycling (stationary)	150	soccer	360
aerobic dancing	200	swimming	265
watching TV	45	tennis	225
walking (5.5 mph)	190	basketball	345

Complete the chart below to keep a record of the exercise you do for one week.

	Type of Exercise(s)	Length of Time (Minutes)	Approximate Calories Burned
Sunday	Answers will vary.		
Monday			
Tuesday			
Wednesday			
Thursday			
Friday			
Saturday			

Answer Key

Name_____

Medicine Labels

The labels on medicine containers give important information. Labels should always be read carefully.

Read the information on the cough medicine labels below. Answer the questions.

Recommended Dosage
Children (5–12 years): 1 teaspoon every 6 hours
Adults: 2 teaspoons every 6 hours
Caution: *Do not administer to children under 5. No more than 4 dosages per day. This product may cause drowsiness; use caution if operating machinery or driving a vehicle. Should not be taken if you are pregnant or nursing a child.*

If cough or fever persists, consult a physician.
Exp. Date: 8/2020

6-hour Cough Relief
Fast, effective relief for coughs due to colds and flu

1. What is the adult dosage? __2 teaspoons every 6 hours__

2. What is a child's dosage? __1 teaspoon every 6 hours__

3. What is a side effect of this medicine? __drowsiness__

4. Who should not take this medicine? __children under 5, pregnant women, and nursing mothers__

5. How many dosages per day can be taken safely? __4__

6. What is the expiration date of this medicine? __August 2020__

7. What action should be taken if the medicine does not relieve your cough?
__consult a physician__

8. For what symptoms should this medicine be taken?
__cough due to cold or flu__

Name_____

Poisons

Children can be very curious. They love to touch things and pick them up. Very young children like to put things into their mouths. What action should be taken if a child swallows a poisonous material?

Read the following safety procedures.

CALL YOUR POISON CONTROL CENTER, HOSPITAL, PHYSICIAN, OR EMERGENCY PHONE NUMBER IMMEDIATELY!

If you cannot obtain emergency advice, follow these procedures.

• If the poison is **corrosive** (paint remover, household cleaners, gasoline, drain opener, ammonia, or lye), **DO NOT** make the patient vomit. Give the patient water or milk to dilute the poison.

• If the poison is **not corrosive** (insect spray, aspirin, pesticides, or medicine), **make the patient vomit** or use a poison control kit. To force the patient to vomit, touch the back of his or her throat.

Place a **V** on each picture that shows poison that should be vomited if swallowed. Circle each poison that should not be vomited if swallowed.
